BOBBIE ANN MASON

A Study of the Short Fiction

Also available in Twayne's Studies in Short Fiction Series

Twayne publishes studies of all major short-story writers worldwide. For a complete list, contact the Publisher directly.

Twayne's Studies in Short Fiction

Gary Scharnhorst and Eric Haralson, General Editors

BOBBIE ANN MASON
Thomas Victor

BOBBIE ANN MASON

A Study of the Short Fiction

Albert Wilhelm
Tennessee Technological University

TWAYNE PUBLISHERS
An Imprint of Simon & Schuster Macmillan
New York

PRENTICE HALL INTERNATIONAL
London Mexico City New Delhi Singapore Sydney Toronto

Twayne's Studies in Short Fiction Series, No. 74

Copyright © 1998 by Twayne Publishers

Twayne Publishers
An Imprint of Simon & Schuster Macmillan
1633 Broadway
New York, NY 10019

Library of Congress Cataloging-in-Publication Data

Wilhelm, Albert.
  Bobbie Ann Mason : a study of the short fiction / Albert Wilhelm.
    p.   cm. (Twayne's studies in short fiction ; no. 74)
  Includes bibliographical references and index.
  ISBN 0-8057-1670-X (alk. paper)
    1. Mason, Bobbie Ann—Criticism and interpretation. 2. Women and literature—United States—History—20th century. 3. Kentucky—In literature. 4. Short story. I. Title. II. Series.
  PS3563.A7877Z95   1998
  813'.54—dc21   98-26220
                                                                          CIP

This paper meets the requirements of ANSI/NISO Z3948-1992 (Permanence of Paper).

10 9 8 7 6 5 4 3 2

Printed in the United States of America

To Pat and Matthew,
fellow lovers of words

Contents

Preface

Bobbie Ann Mason's career as a writer of fiction started late but soon flourished. Although she began writing stories as an undergraduate, she soon detoured into journalism (features for *Movie Life* magazine) and, at the other extreme, into academic writing (a scholarly study of Nabokov's *Ada*). Except for one early story in a student literary magazine, her first published fiction was "Offerings" in the 18 February 1980 issue of the *New Yorker*. The story "Shiloh" also appeared in the *New Yorker* a few months later and provoked a flurry of favorable responses. This story so impressed Amanda Urban of International Creative Management that she called Mason and offered to become her agent.

In 1982 "Shiloh" became the lead selection in Mason's first volume of collected stories, *Shiloh and Other Stories*. This book received high praise from reviewers such as Anne Tyler and Raymond Carver. It won the Ernest Hemingway award (for the year's most notable first fiction) and was nominated for the American Book Award and the National Book Critics Circle Award.

Mason's reputation has continued to rise with the publication of three novels—*In Country* (1985), *Spence + Lila* (1988), *Feather Crowns* (1993)—and another volume of stories, *Love Life* (1989). As evidence of her acceptance into the academic canon, most of the standard anthologies for courses in short fiction or American literature now include at least one story by Mason. Essays on Mason's work began to appear in scholarly journals as early as 1985, and the body of criticism is now small but significant. Discussion of a few stories in *Shiloh and Other Stories* has been extensive, while commentary on those in *Love Life* remains relatively sparse. Part 1 of this volume will expand earlier criticism by providing analysis of 12 of the 16 selections from *Shiloh and Other Stories* and 12 of the 15 stories from *Love Life*. Part 2 contains a new interview with Mason provided especially for this volume, along with excerpts from an earlier interview from *Contemporary Literature*. Part 3 provides the complete texts of two of the most significant scholarly essays on Mason's short fiction.

I am grateful to Bobbie Ann Mason and Roger Rawlings, her husband, for their gracious cooperation in the preparation of this volume; to Tennessee Technological University for its grant of released time and other assistance in preparing my manuscript; to my colleagues Wanda Jared, Carroll Viera, Shirley Laird, Helen Deese, and Jim Akenson for their advice and encouragement; to my son Matthew for information about references to popular music in Mason's stories; and especially to my wife Pat for her enduring support.

Acknowledgments

"An Interview with Bobbie Ann Mason" conducted by Bonnie Lyons and Bill Oliver first appeared in *Contemporary Literature* 32 (1991): 449–70. © 1991 by the University of Wisconsin Press. Reprinted by permission.

"Bobbie Ann Mason and the Recovery of Mystery" by Richard Giannone first appeared in *Studies in Short Fiction* 27 (Fall 1990): 553–66. © 1990 by Newberry College. Reprinted by permission.

"The Function of Popular Culture in Bobbie Ann Mason's *Shiloh and Other Stories* and *In Country*" by Leslie White first appeared in *Southern Quarterly* 26 (Summer 1988): 69–79. © 1988 by the University of Southern Mississippi. Reprinted by permission.

The frontispiece photograph of Bobbie Ann Mason © by Thomas Victor.

Part 1

THE SHORT FICTION

Introduction

A perceptive reviewer has compared the typical Bobbie Ann Mason story to "a meal of collard greens and Big Macs."[1] Such a menu mixes the old-fashioned with the newfangled, the down-home country with the increasingly urban, the distinctively regional with the blandly regionless, and these same tensions are central to Mason's short fiction. In "The Climber," for example, the main character listens to "Elvira" on the radio and recalls that the Oak Ridge Boys "used to be a gospel quartet" but have suddenly become a trendy group "with blow-dried hair, singing country-rock songs about love."[2] In "Love Life" a spinster schoolteacher scorns traditional needlework and sits enthralled by the rapidly "morphing" images on MTV. In "Lying Doggo" a young woman removed from her rural roots observes: "One day I was listening to Hank Williams and shelling corn for the chickens and the next day I was expected to know what wines went with what" (*S*, 207).

The facts of Mason's own life tell a similar story of social anomalies and culture shock. She grew up on a small dairy farm near Mayfield, Kentucky, where she "picked blackberries" and "hoed vegetables in the scorching morning sun," but she was hooked into the larger world through the music on WLAC radio.[3] During her teen years she served as national president of the Hilltoppers fan club and traveled to their concerts in faraway places like Detroit and St. Louis. After graduating from college, she ventured even farther away from her country home. As a writer for *Movie Life* magazine in New York City, she interviewed glamorous teen stars like Ann-Margret, Annette Funicello, and Fabian. Eventually Mason returned to graduate school and earned a Ph.D. in English with a dissertation on a remarkably sophisticated expatriate, Vladimir Nabokov. Mason then taught briefly at Mansfield State College in Pennsylvania. Now, her own prize-winning stories are studied on campuses all over the country.

From this highly charged mix of pop and high culture, pastoral simplicity and urban sophistication, Mason draws her creative energies. Just as Mason experienced cultural dislocation as she grew up, her characters must also confront the disturbing consequences of rapid social change in their life passages. In a 1985 interview Mason commented: "I'm constantly preoccupied with . . . exploring various kinds of culture shock—people moving from one class to another . . . people being threatened by other people's ways and values."[4] In other interviews Mason has discussed the breakdown of family and one's sense of place and the resulting difficulty in "retaining identity and integrity."[5]

Scholarly commentaries on Mason's stories echo her own statements. One critic observes that "Mason's characters live in a protean world of rapid, dizzying change." Trying to find their identities "in the midst of constant flux, they seek to discover something to hold on to in this modern emotional environment," where familiar rituals disappear and old social patterns disintegrate.[6] Another scholar says that Mason's characters are "overwhelmed by rapid and frightening changes" and "must confront contradictory impulses, the temptation to withdraw into the security of home and the past, and the alternative prospect of taking to the road in search of something better."[7]

Almost all of Mason's collected stories are set in or near small western Kentucky towns that R. Z. Sheppard has termed "ruburbs." These schizophrenic places that are "no longer rural but not yet suburban" mirror the confusion of their residents.[8] Small towns like Hopewell may still be home to Mason's characters, but interstate highways quickly lure them away to Louisville, Nashville, Memphis, and St. Louis. Indeed, the dominant forces are centrifugal, and lives spin outward and away. Mason's stories may appear to have a cohesive nucleus, like the extended family gathering for Christmas dinner in "Drawing Names," but this core frequently crumbles and dissipates.

Even if Mason's literary landscape is a postmodernist ruburb where centers cannot hold, her impulse as a writer remains more traditional and at times even approaches the pastoral. Fully aware of the confusion in the world around her, in many of her stories she still seeks a vision of order, wholeness, and unity with the natural world.

Mark A. R. Facknitz has commented that no contemporary writer willingly accepts the minimalist label because it may suggest narrowness of vision.[9] Even so, the term is frequently applied to Mason's work, and her stories are sometimes linked with those of Raymond Carver, "the chief practitioner of what's been called 'American minimalism.' "[10] To understand the relevance of this label to Mason's fiction, one must distinguish among several senses of the word. In 1985 a double issue of the *Mississippi Review* focused exclusively on minimalism, but its contributors failed to agree on an entirely satisfactory definition. An essay by John

Barth, considered by many the best commentary on the subject, identifies several varieties of minimalism. Barth begins with "minimalisms of unit, form and scale," which are displayed in strikingly short paragraphs or entire stories (sometimes called "sudden fictions," "minute fictions," or "flash fictions" because of their extreme brevity).[11] Such minimalisms of form may or may not coincide with minimalisms of style—"a stripped-down vocabulary; a stripped-down syntax that avoids periodic sentences" (Barth, 8–9). Finally, Barth posits minimalisms of materials as found in stories with few characters, little exposition, limited action, and negligible plot (9).

Some critics of contemporary fiction have gone further to identify and decry what might be termed a "minimalism of teleology." Stories of this sort display characters apparently bereft of any spiritual values moving aimlessly through a moral void. The "perfect economy" of this extreme minimalism strips away moral involvement by author and reader, suggesting that "the writer's responsibility is only to register what is true in a literal, documentary sense."[12] According to Madison Bell such reductionism produces "an excessively small" literary community whose members cultivate "an obsessive concern for surface detail, a tendency to ignore or eliminate distinctions among people it renders, and a studiedly deterministic, at times nihilistic, vision of the world."[13] As characterized by Bell, the minimalist story may sound like a much terser and more carefully controlled reincarnation of the naturalistic fiction produced by Theodore Dreiser and Jack London.

Given this profusion of minimalisms, one must ask which specific manifestations are present in Mason's stories and how the concept can help to illuminate her work. Mason is clearly not a minimalist of form and scale. None of her collected stories are flash fictions, and even the shortest runs well over 3,000 words. Mason's work does exhibit some of the qualities identified by Barth as characteristic of minimalism in style and materials, and she once commented jokingly that she limits herself to a vocabulary of only 600 words.[14] Mason asserts that she is "not trying to be a minimalist"; she is merely "expressing the terse, compact language" of her region.[15] She says that she shies away "from making large statements" because she distrusts them.[16]

Even with these limitations, her stories cannot be diminished to the kind of minimalism described by Bell. To the extent that Mason is a minimalist, her adherence to that school is methodological rather than teleological. In the tradition of Hemingway, she avoids unnecessary embellishments; she uses minimalism as a means of drawing "the boundaries of truth" and concerns herself "only with the matter that lies within" (Facknitz, 63). Nevertheless, Mason is emphatically concerned with truth, and her "matter" is never a moral void. Far from being reductive, her stories, according to Richard Giannone, emphasize "the recovery of mystery." Giannone argues that Mason is much more than an astute "chronicler of how we live." Indeed, she "is alive to the distant, unseen dimension of life." Even though her characters live in confused places and dispiriting times, they persistently seek and sometimes find evidence that "their lives add up to something beyond themselves."[17]

Mason has frequently proclaimed her own fascination with puzzles and mysteries. As a child she loved the challenge of putting together the pieces of a jigsaw puzzle, and she later progressed to helping her grandmother assemble the puzzlelike pieces of patchwork quilt squares. Her primary reading materials were adolescent detective stories where girl sleuths like Judy Bolton, Cherry Ames, and Nancy Drew sought clues, sorted evidence, and solved mysteries. In these early activities Mason sees the stimulus for her later development as a student and creator of literature. In 1994 in a preface for a new edition of *The Girl Sleuth,* she wrote: "The combination of all those influences led me to delight in the intricate design of fiction. I'm still a girl sleuth, setting my magnifying glass onto words and images and the great mysteries of life."[18]

In so casually comparing herself to Nancy Drew and other girl sleuths, Mason reveals sharp differences between herself and extreme minimalists. Mason perceives the world around her not as a moral void but as a realm of mysteries to be explored. As a literary artist she creates not just documentary accounts of despair but carefully wrought fictions with their own intricate designs. Within these stories most of Mason's protagonists share her teleological impulse. Like her, they attempt to fit together pieces of the puzzle, to see the pattern, to comprehend the mystery.

In their various teleological gropings Mason's characters display three basic sorts of behavior. Some are travelers escaping constrained environments and hitting the road in search of purpose. A few characters remain at home to cultivate their gardens and thus attempt to find order within the patterns of nature. Still other characters are craftspeople and aspiring artists who try to compose their lives by assembling random parts into a coherent whole.

Travelers and Pilgrims: Looking for Love, Purpose, and Fulfillment in Many of the Wrong Places

In Mason's novel *In Country*, a homesick soldier in Vietnam has a map of western Kentucky tattooed on his chest. Pete Simms's tattoo shows the entire Jackson Purchase area and even includes the street in front of his house and a tiny red dot representing his Corvette. This area of Kentucky—small enough for a detailed map to fit on Pete's chest—is home to Mason and most of the characters in her stories. The region's limited size and insular nature once offered security and reassurance. In the contemporary context of Mason's stories, however, boundaries between home and the larger world are blurred, and forces of change challenge the stability of old ways.

In a *New Yorker* essay entitled "The Way We Lived," Mason describes the Jackson Purchase area in detail. Bought from Chinubby, king of the Chickasaw nation, in 1818, the territory is a 2,500-square-mile peninsula. Surrounded on three sides by large lakes and rivers, it connects to land only along the Tennessee border. Mason's great-great-great-grandfather, Samuel Mason, was one of the earliest settlers in the Cumberland River region of Tennessee, and soon after the Jackson Purchase two of his children moved into that area to establish the Clear Springs community on Panther Creek. From that time and place, says Mason, sprang all the relatives she has ever known.[19]

Although Mason's family was deeply rooted in the soil of western Kentucky, powerful forces lured her and many others of her generation away from home. Just west of the Mason family farm was U.S. Highway 45, a thin ribbon of asphalt that linked provincial Mayfield to Chicago in the North or Tupelo, Mississippi (the birthplace of Elvis), and Mobile in the South. While cherishing her roots, Mason succumbed to "the allure of rootlessness" ("Way," 88). She writes: "The highway called us too. Our ancestors had been lured over the ocean by false advertising—

7

here was the promised land, literally—but, once arrived they had to clear stumps and learn to raise hogs instead of sheep. We inherited their gullibility. We wanted to go places, find out what was out there" (94).

Even as Mason and her contemporaries traveled away from home, inbound traffic also produced dramatic alterations. Today Mayfield sits at the intersection of U.S. Highway 45 and the Purchase Parkway, and Mason describes her family farm as the hub of the area's industrial growth. Of this economic development and its attendant social change Mason writes: "The tension between holding on to a way of life and letting in a new way of life—under the banners of Wal-Marts and chicken processors—is the central dynamic of this area. There are no malls, no cineplexes, no coffee bars here and none are likely any time soon. But a Wal-Mart Supercenter is coming. The town is poised on the edge of the future" ("Way," 96–97).

Since most of Mason's stories are set in her home territory, critics have commented frequently on her regionalism. One reviewer describes *Shiloh and Other Stories* as a picture of the Old South rapidly becoming the New South.[20] Mason readily acknowledges her Southern heritage and observes that the Purchase area, more so than other parts of Kentucky, "historically and temperamentally . . . looks to the South" ("Way," 88). At the same time she professes to know very little about Southern history and says she never thinks "about the Southern literary tradition" (Shomer, 89). Unlike many Southern writers Mason did not "grow up hearing stories" and was never a part of the great regional "storytelling tradition" (Havens, 90).

We can see the limits of Mason's regionalism by visualizing the geography of her native region. The Jackson Purchase is a stumpy appendage protruding northward a few miles from the Deep South. Mason's characters can easily drive to Corinth, Mississippi, or to Memphis—where, according to local folklore, the Mississippi Delta begins in the lobby of the Peabody Hotel. These characters are in the South, but their geography pulls them away from its heart. Like the people in Faulkner's stories, for example, they are concerned with family and tradition, but they are largely oblivious to the specific heritage of racial injustice and defeat in the Civil War. These weighty issues, which define so many characters and determine so much of the action in classic Southern fiction, are insignificant in Mason's stories.

Insofar as Mason is a Southern regional writer, she is concerned less with place than with process. She examines the Purchase area not as a special site rich in local color but as a crucible of change—the same sort of change that is taking place to some degree all over the country. To be sure, the characters and idioms of her early stories seemed decidedly exotic to typical readers of the *New Yorker*, and Mason herself has remarked facetiously that her subject was "Southern Gothic goes to the supermarket" (Havens, 90). This joke in itself suggests Mason's primary focus—difficulties in transition that may be exacerbated by regional differences. As noted earlier, the Purchase area is peninsular in form, and it was for many years insular in outlook. Since much of the South remained for so long isolated and resistant to change, the onset there of radical social changes seems all the more dramatic and their progress more disruptive. Thus, with cataclysmic bursts of change in the late twentieth century, Mason's regional crucible is especially volatile. Amidst all this activity Mason's characters move uneasily about the area and sometimes travel beyond it in simple flight or in more purposeful trips of exploration. According to Allen Tate and Lewis Lawson, the force that radically altered the South was not the Civil War but the development of highways.[21] The actions of many Mason characters document this dramatic change.

Throughout history travel has been an important index of social change and a frequent response to it. Obviously recent decades have brought an explosion of opportunities for travel and have dramatically accelerated its pace. Before 1890 humans had never attained a speed of 100 miles per hour, but only 80 years later the Concorde began routine flights reaching 1,320 miles per hour and space capsules orbited the earth at speeds in excess of 17,000 miles per hour.[22] Mason's characters are not jet-setters, but their travels are frequent—in cars, trucks, speedboats, and occasionally airplanes. In several stories such travel is a significant means of character revelation and narrative development.

In most cases travel involves much more than simple linear progression from point A to point B. Through the ages men and women have traveled for highly diverse reasons—to explore the unknown, to convert the heathen, to make profit through trade or conquest, to renew physical or spiritual health. Whatever the original motive, travel may have unexpected results. Joan Corwin defines a "travel experience" as "the inevitable confrontation of the self and its cultural baggage with the foreign other." Thus, travel becomes a "trial of identity," a challenge to the traveler's sense of self.[23] Travel for a Mason character is seldom extensive or exotic, but it does help to define the individual—to clarify his or her place on the map of a changing world.

Some of Mason's less successful protagonists simply occupy the roads in or near their hometowns, substituting aimless motion for the boredom or pain of a fixed place. (Mason notes that one of her first stories, which remains unpublished, was entitled "Running Around" [Dorothy Hill, 108].) Other characters travel more determinedly within western Kentucky, Illinois, and Tennessee, stretching the boundaries of home and just beginning to overcome its constraints. Still other characters make more-extended pilgrimages with varying degrees of success. For example, the young protagonist in "Detroit Skyline, 1949" gains important though incomplete insights through her journey to the North. In a very different case the retired couple in "The Ocean" journey to a supposed shrine but find it empty. For one group of Mason's characters travel is recursive. Having explored the larger world, they return home to examine old values in light of their new experiences.

"Midnight Magic" (1987)

One of the most aimless of Mason's local travelers is the protagonist of "Midnight Magic." This young man is called Steve, but a customized car—his automotive alter ego—bears the more flamboyant name "Midnight Magic" emblazoned in all the colors of the rainbow on its rear end. Steve, an adult in years but still a child emotionally, appears pallid beside this technicolor extravaganza, and his powers as a man can hardly match those of the internal combustion engine. In keeping with her emphasis on travel, Mason begins and ends her story with detailed images of the car. Like its owner the automobile is a turbocharged vehicle with no clear destination, a pulsing motor with no notion of how its energies should be engaged. Furthermore, Steve's erratic physical travel in and around his hometown parallels his confused and truncated journey of personal development.

In his fascination with automobiles, Steve recalls the adolescent males in Breece D'J Pancake's stories about small-town life in West Virginia. For Pancake's financially strapped shade-tree mechanics, the primary task is getting a wreck of a car off blocks and onto the highway. Like Steve, however, they invest the automobile with magical powers. Far more than a means of travel, the car becomes in their high-flown dreams a vehicle for sexual maturation, personal fulfillment, and spiritual liberation.

Actually, Steve's obsession with the car is itself an indication of his arrested emotional development. His juvenile preoccupation with the powerful machine suggests a retreat into autoeroticism, and even when he thinks about his girlfriend Karen, automotive values govern his response.

Karen's "working knowledge of crankshafts and fuel pumps" ranks high on his list of her most attractive qualities.[24]

Since Steve is unable to love Karen as an adult, he typically resorts to adolescent games. In her kitchen "he turns to box playfully at her" (*LL*, 25), and Mason's choice of prepositions obviously indicates distance rather than togetherness in the relationship. In his apartment he tousles her hair and pulls her down on the sofa to tickle her. In insisting that he is "just playing" (20), Steve reveals a truth more comprehensive than he realizes. Such play displays boyish energy far more appropriate to the schoolyard than to a mature relationship. Steve is obviously puzzled about how to channel masculine power into a fitting demonstration of love, and Karen senses in his confusion an ominous potential for violence. She compares him to a cat that gets rough during play and actually wants to rip apart a rabbit. Steve seems domesticated, but, like his car, he could become feral without warning.

Mason explores this feral aspect of Steve's character by including in the story several potential doubles. One that invites close comparison with Steve is a mysterious rapist who has struck twice in Karen's neighborhood. This grim double recalls Mason's comments on the genesis of "Midnight Magic." Her inspiration for the story was a young man sitting in his car drinking chocolate milk and eating chocolate-covered doughnuts. In spite of this childish food, the strange man "looked like he could be a rapist and really mean." In writing her story Mason kept trying "to tone him down"—to modulate between a character who was "too nice" and one "just totally out of control."[25] In the finished story Steve becomes a feckless but engaging character. The rapist, however, lingers as an ominous echo—the penumbral image of an identity that Steve has barely avoided.

Vestigial traces of his literary evolution still cling to Steve, and his amiable behavior may suddenly turn atavistic. At one point in the story, Steve angers Karen by pretending to be the rapist, and he later imagines in detail how he might act out the role of male dominator. Ironically, Steve's reverie contains a curious shift in perspective that further reveals his confusion. He starts out as the aggressor but soon "shudders" (*LL*, 28), steps out of that character, and becomes a bystander in his own fantasy while the unknown rapist continues the action.

If Steve perceives Karen as an antagonist rather than a mate, his casual relationships with other women are also frequently combative. In the laundromat, for example, he competes with a female customer for the use of a dryer. In an effort to awe this woman, he tells a feeble joke suggesting that Ronald Reagan bombed Libya to impress Jodie Foster. This oblique reference to the John Hinckley assassination attempt introduces an ominous subtext and another potential double for Steve. Of course, Steve's behavior is far less extreme than Hinckley's. Like Hinckley, however, he is painfully eager to impress women and woefully ignorant of how to do so except by a display of power.

When Steve sees women as antagonists, courting becomes combat, but at times, as a static alternative to violence, he places women on lofty but unsteady pedestals. For example, he tells himself that Nancy, the new wife of his best friend Doran, will "be an immaculate house-keeper," and in her domain everything will "be clean and pretty and safe" (*LL*, 28).

Caught between two false notions of love—unacceptable adolescent violence and an unrealistic ideal—Steve can do little more than circle aimlessly. Marshall Blonsky describes American democracy as "freedom conceived spatially"—an ethos that has in time fostered the primacy of the automobile.[26] Historically this spatial freedom took the form of a clear vector. From wagon trains moving steadily westward to Corvettes cruising along Route 66, such movement was both unrestrained and unambiguously directional. In Steve's case, however, the car repeatedly traces a circular pattern throughout the town as he travels to the laundromat, to Karen's apartment, back to the laundromat, to Karen's apartment again, and once more to the laundromat. Steve finally breaks out of this tight circle to head to the Nashville airport where he is supposed to pick up Doran and Nancy, returning from their honeymoon at Disney World. Ironically, he is several hours late in starting out to meet their plane, just as he is several years tardy in maturing. The story never shows Steve arriving at his geographic destination, and he is even less likely to reach his own fantasyland of safety and peace with a Stepford wife.

On the interstate to Nashville, Steve encounters still another potential double and an ominous warning about the dangers of his aimless travel. In this case the double wears running shoes reminiscent of Steve's but lies facedown near the road like a dead man or a bag full of trash. The immobile figure with no car nearby becomes an emblem of Steve's condition apart from his powerful automobile. Like the body near the shoulder of the road, Steve is on the margins of life. If Steve expends all his energies in confused circular movement, he may indeed be left stranded like the motionless body.

Despite the power of his car, Steve becomes immobilized in his quest for love because he "wants something miraculous" but simply "can't believe in it" (*LL*, 29). His life dramatizes a persistent hope yoked with an elusive faith, and such a combination inevitably produces frustration. Steve feels angry at other searchers in the story who are moderately successful in their quests. His brother Bud has sought and found his prize dog, Big Red. Karen has found transcendent meaning in the spiritual teachings of Sardo, an ancient American Indian now reincarnated in the body of a teenager. In contrast to these modest but significant quests, Steve merely searches for laundry and thinks Karen must have hidden it. He "spends half his life chasing after his clothes" (25), and after making three trips to the laundromat to wash and dry them, he leaves town without ever removing them from the machine.

Mason ends the story with Steve inside a cramped phone booth calling an emergency number to report the body he has seen. Unfortunately the 911 operator is an intimidating woman who asks the straightforward but surprisingly difficult question, "Where are you, sir?" (*LL*, 32). Steve cannot articulate an adequate response defining either his precise geographic location or his larger position in life. As he looks through spread fingers at tiny segments of scenery, his view of the world is limited and disconnected. Once again he focuses exclusively on his car still idling impatiently outside the phone booth. Steve's potential for movement is obvious, but the proper direction remains as mysterious as midnight magic.

Lagging behind in his personal development, Steve illustrates a more pervasive cultural lag. The car remains a primary icon of American freedom, but its potency as a symbol is steadily eroding. According to Marshall Blonsky, we have moved beyond the automobile generation to "the telematic, the culture of will projectible over distance." In this new age space becomes irrelevant because we can "forage far from our roots" using "nomadic objects" like fax machines, cellular phones, and laptop computers. Thus, "to the telematic nomad, a car is pure nostalgia, a sign of a lost time." In the phone booth at the conclusion of this story, Steve is hooked loosely into the telematic age but he remains totally committed to the automotive. Adoring his beautiful automobile to the end, Steve may well be one of the last to realize that the "Mighty Car, the Phallomobile, is finished" (Blonsky, 27).

"Sorghum" (1988)

Two recurring activities in the story "Sorghum" are driving and eating. For the most part, however, the trips reach no significant destinations and the consumption of food fails to satisfy a pervasive hunger.

13

"Sorghum" begins with a flamboyant display of automotive power much like that in "Midnight Magic." Now the automobile driver is a husband and father of two with a responsible job at the local tire plant. Although Danny in "Sorghum" is several years older than Steve in "Midnight Magic," he is only slightly more mature. Unhappy in his marriage and seething with repressed anger, Danny roars into his driveway, noisily backs out again, and tears through the subdivision with tires screeching and squealing. Although the hour is three in the morning, Danny repeats this routine several times before slamming the car door and announcing loudly, "I'm home" (*LL*, 199). Danny's early-morning "joy ride" (198) is, in fact, joyless. His frantic journey ends exactly where it began—at a "home" that is ironically falling apart.

Although Danny is not the central character of "Sorghum," his nocturnal forays serve as an appropriate prologue to the story's main action. Danny speeds away from home but never arrives at any other destination. His wife, Liz, also drives away from their unhappy marriage but discovers no satisfactory alternatives. Liz's movements away from Danny are at first very tentative. She jumps into her car, in this case an underpowered Chevette, and drives aimlessly through town. Although her velocity is much less than Danny's, her route is just as haphazard. Such random movements reflect her confused inner state. She feels "a burning desire, for no one in particular, nothing she knew" (*LL*, 200). In an effort to appease this intense but unspecific desire, Liz decides to satisfy a particular "craving for sorghum" (201). She hasn't eaten this old-fashioned syrup since she was a child, and, merging the motifs of travel and food, she drives several miles out into the country to purchase it.

Although "Sorghum" is Mason's only short story whose title focuses explicitly on food, several other stories deal at least incidentally with the presumed salvific effect of food and cooking. In "Shiloh," for example, as Norma Jean strives to become a new woman she also prepares new dishes. Through the sympathetic magic of these culinary experiments, she apparently hopes to take on the newness of what she eats. In "Drawing Names" the matriarch of an extended family prepares ham, sweet potato balls with marshmallow centers, oriental casserole, and countless other dishes, but this profusion of ritualistic food fails to provide any real communion. Indeed, as an indication of the futility of such efforts, one family member suggests that the feasters will all need stomach bypasses after consuming so much food. Such a meal can lead to excess consumption but no real satisfaction. For Mason's mother and grandmother food "was purpose, its preparation an act of creativity, its giving an affirmation of life."[27] For the characters in Mason's stories, such larger values have begun to erode.

Mason's focus on food in "Sorghum" recalls the popular self-help books by Geneen Roth. In *When Food Is Love* and *Appetites*, Roth discusses the displacement of desires whereby eating becomes a metonymic substitute for friendship, intimacy, and success. Indeed, Roth's subtitle for *Appetites*—*On the Search for True Nourishment*—might be an apt description of Liz's odyssey in "Sorghum." Like other Mason characters Liz can achieve fullness but no fulfillment. The one foodstuff she seeks on her journey may temporarily satisfy her hunger, but its nutritive value is limited and perhaps its sweetness will soon become cloying.

In driving to the country to buy sorghum from an old man who has made the syrup for generations, Liz is also trying to travel back in time. Like Leroy in "Shiloh" or Cleo in "Old Things," she attempts to escape the confusion of the present by reverting to a simpler past, but the good old days are extremely elusive. Instead of mules circling to squeeze juice out of the sorghum cane, here a newly invented machine performs that function. Squatting incongruously near the old vat where the sorghum cooks is a huge, shiny satellite dish. Working alongside Cletus Summer, the old sorghum maker, is his son Ed, who sells high-tech sound equipment in Memphis but returns to help with farmwork from time to time.

At the sorghum vat Liz gets not just an old-fashioned sweet but also a very contemporary lover. By climbing into Ed's red Camaro (far more alluring than her puny Chevette) and taking off with him to Paducah, she initiates her most decisive movement away from Danny. In an attempt to revive her failing marriage, Liz had begged Danny to take her out to eat at an elegant restaurant. Arthur Berger has noted that various foods constitute a semiotic system conferring status and acceptance or disesteem and rejection upon the consumer. Furthermore, the act of "dining out in fancy restaurants is theatre."[28] Since Danny did not satisfy either Liz's specific culinary desires or her more generalized longings, she readily accepts Ed's invitation to go out for her favorite food—ice cream. In comparing typical American food to Mexican and French cuisine, Octavio Paz says that the former emphasizes milk and ice cream and thus reinforces purity and pregenital innocence.[29] Ironically, Liz's drive to Paducah for ice cream leads to more exotic indulgences—margaritas, Cajun chicken, and adultery. In this case food has not necessarily become love, but it has at least metamorphosed into sex.

During the next few weeks Liz adeptly blends driving, eating, and romance. She drives to the mall, meets Ed there for a meal, and then proceeds to his single bed back at the farm. Their lovemaking there is "like a car going into fifth gear" (*LL,* 207), and this fast sex apparently displaces Liz's urge to travel and explore. With all his superficial charms, however, Ed cannot provide the nourishment she seeks. He admits that his own life is "dangerous and unfulfilled" (205), and, like a fast car or instant pudding, his major virtue is speed.

Liz and Ed meet at the sorghum-cooking vat, but the story ends after a trip to a fancy dinner party in an elegant house on Reelfoot Lake. Ed takes Liz to this traditional wild-game dinner because it is "supposed to mean something" (*LL,* 207). In fact, the food here is abundant, but this shared meal is bereft of any larger values. Liz does indeed learn at this party even though the meaning she derives from the experience is hardly what Ed had expected. Liz immediately feels uncomfortable among Ed's pretentious friends and sees phoniness all around her. For example, her host wears a dinner jacket made from camouflage material, his voice sounds like the artificial tones produced by a mechanical toy, and his den is filled with shelves of duck decoys. The dinner menu is itself further evidence of artificiality. The wild-game dishes presumably reflect the past, but most of these meats are actually out of season and remain available for eating all at one time only because of modern techniques for freezing. Furthermore, at this effete dinner the wildness of each dish is elegantly disguised. The rabbit has been pickled, the quail stuffed with liver, the goose covered with cream sauce, and the duck flavored with cherries. Since wild-game dishes are old-fashioned, they should evoke solid traditional values—what Liz sought at the sorghum vat. Since such foods are now exotic, their semiotic values should also reflect elegance and high status. In this strange mix of sauce and substance, however, the overall message is garbled and incoherent. The entire meal reminds Liz of a painting she once saw. This beautiful picture showed "a fantasy mixture of flowers throughout the seasons, from the early-spring hyacinths to the fall asters" (213). Such a fantastic bouquet could be contrived in a painting but never in real life.

By the end of "Sorghum," Liz has taken many trips in Ed's red Camaro, but she has not yet found an appropriate route beyond her failed marriage to Danny. Having traveled extensively between Paducah and Reelfoot Lake, having sampled sorghum, Cajun chicken, and a vast array of wild game, she still finds nothing to her taste. In response to the basic question, "What did she really want?" (*LL,* 213), she can only reply that she does not know.

Liz's dilemma is similar to one that Mason says she experiences in a recurring dream. In an interview with Dorothy Combs Hill, Mason observes:

I have always had anxiety and difficulty choosing foods. All my life I've had these food dreams. The dream is that I'm in something like the Marriott buffet trying to figure out what to eat, because there's all this beautiful food. All the foods in the world, and I can have anything I want, and I work and work at choosing these foods, and fill my plate up. It takes forever. And then I wake up . . . I don't get to eat it. And then, a few years ago, when I started publishing my stories, I started having food dreams in which I got to eat the food. I hadn't realized that it would still throw me in a panic to actually go through a buffet line. I mean, I walked around all that time just looking at it. And I always manage to choose the wrong things. I wish I'd chosen something else. (Dorothy Hill, 113)

Mason has also described her teenage work experience at a drugstore soda fountain (where she could have all the Cokes and ice cream she wanted) as a "mini-version of the buffet line" (Dorothy Hill, 114). Offered more than she could ever consume, she became unable even to choose.

Even if Liz has not yet found the food that nourishes her—the remedy for her spiritual bulimia—the artificiality of the wild-game dinner has helped her to see what she does not want and what she cannot realistically expect to have. The dinner and its attendant image of the contrived painting serve as powerful reminders that for everything there is a season. Liz's late-summer romance with Ed Summer has by now proceeded past its season and into the autumn. This affair is no doubt destined to end shortly, but Liz feels that something important is about to happen in her life. As the story concludes, she has locked herself inside a steamy greenhouse equipped with a Jacuzzi. She has never before seen a hot tub, but she carefully removes her stockings and dress and cautiously sticks one toe into the bubbling water. Not yet prepared to plunge in, Liz does test the waters. The story suggests that in due time she will be ready to emerge from the artificial environment of the greenhouse into a new season of personal growth.

"Memphis" (1988)

Beverly, the main character in "Memphis," happens to see a bumper sticker proclaiming "A WOMAN'S PLACE IS IN THE MALL" (*LL*, 226). Within this feeble joke is a significant comment on Beverly's quest for identity. On the road in search of meaning, she risks being detoured into a shopping center parking lot. Rather than discovering her inner resources, she may simply amass more goods. Beverly's basic problem is much like that of Liz in "Sorghum." The shopper may overfill her closet just as the victim of bulimia may overfill her stomach, but both remain profoundly unsatisfied.

At many points in history, the line between quest and acquisition, between travel and consumerism, has become blurred. In the sixteenth century, for example, European explorers promptly planted flags and claimed parts of the mysterious New World as the property of their respective monarchs. Today's tourists may glance at various natural and artistic wonders of the world, then proceed immediately to the nearby gift shops. Instead of experiencing the marvel to which they have traveled, they try to own at least a semblance of it.

Mason observes that this phenomenon is deeply ingrained in American culture. She writes: "The American dream is the desire to absorb, know, and conquer everything, to go everywhere and to do it all, and to take whatever is free, even if you can't use it. We even have eating contests to show off our gluttony." Describing America when first discovered by Europeans as "a consumer's paradise," she says that "the settlers came over here and saw this whole banquet of beautiful land and their eyes were bigger than their stomachs and so they chopped down more than they could use and called it the United States" (*Sleuth*, 45–46). In *Spence + Lila* Mason comments on this ever-accelerating excess. After walking through the aisles of Wal-Mart, Spence observes: "People are buying so much junk, thinking it will make them happy. And when they can't even make a path across the floor through their possessions, they have a yard sale."[30].

"Memphis" provides a dramatic example of middle-class consumerism run amuck. All around her Beverly sees a profusion of motor vehicles. Her ex-husband Joe and his friends own fleets of motorcycles, three-wheelers, cars, and trucks, but, even with all these wheels, they seldom go anywhere. These oxymoronic vehicles that remain essentially static show that the basic problem in this story is not a deficiency of means but an absence of purpose, not a lack of opportunity to travel forward but the inability to choose wisely among alternatives.

Continuing the conceit of aborted travel, Beverly sees her ex-husband and herself as two cars "stalled at a crossroads, each thinking the other had the right-of-way" (*LL*, 224). This metaphor of interrupted movement captures nicely the static quality of Beverly's life. Divorced for a year, she still lives only eight blocks from Joe, still finds him sexy, and still sleeps with him on occasion. Unable to make a clean break with the past, Beverly cannot move toward or even define her new role.

In an effort to travel beyond these confused circumstances, Beverly at first goes only as far as the tanning salon run by her friend Jolene. Here she can crawl into the tanning bed, close her eyes, and see pictures from within as she meditates. In fact, she views the tanning cubicle as a fantasy transporter—a tiny spaceship that can beam her up to another world. She speculates that in the future people will get inside a contraption much like this and "go time traveling, unbounded by time and space or custody arrangements" (*LL*, 223). Unfortunately, Beverly sets this liberating travel in the future rather than in the present, in fantasy rather than in actuality. Beverly's fears overcome the allure of any such voyages of exploration. Instead of using her free weekends for trips of discovery, she regards them as black holes—vast empty spaces that will suck her in.

Even though the tanning bed promises freedom, Beverly gives it a grim name. In calling it "the sunshine coffin" (*LL*, 223), she may be alluding to the possibility that its rays will cause skin cancer. In another sense this oxymoronic phrase may be an oblique comment on Beverly's difficult transition from wife to single mother. Like several other Mason characters she falls "between one thing and another"; she lives "in an absence bracketed by nostalgia and apprehension."[31] Only when her old relationship with Joe is finally pronounced dead and buried in its coffin can she finally emerge into the sunshine of a new life.

When Beverly eventually ventures out on a real trip rather than an imaginary one, her destination is Memphis. As she and Jolene take off for a weekend in that city, Jolene cries out, "Elvis, we're on our way, baby" (*LL*, 225). This spirited invocation reminds us that Memphis was the scene of one fabulous success story and suggests that other grand opportunities await. Mason describes the city as a cornucopia of options. Driving down the highway, the two women pass a Kmart, a Wal-Mart, and a host of other emporia, and Jolene assures Beverly that a particular record store in Memphis has "everything you could name, going way back to the very beginning" (225). Even a mundane Walgreen's store in Memphis amazes Beverly with its profusion of hair-care products.

In painting Memphis as a place of freedom and limitless possibilities, Beverly and Jolene may be investing far too much hope in this pop-culture mecca. In commenting on our culture of plenty, Orin Klapp has noted that along with abundance comes inflation and inevitable loss of value. Intellectual and spiritual inflation occur, he says, "when too many symbols have too little meaning."[32] Charles Newman also discusses "the devaluation of all received ideas" in postmodern culture. In a time when "chronic excess demand fosters irrational consumption," then "all goods, intellectual as well as material, become nondurable."[33] Amidst all the goods around her, Beverly can find few valuable resources and little true wealth.

As one example of this postmodern devaluation of symbols, Mason includes in "Memphis" an ironic reappropriation of a venerable icon. On one occasion when Beverly visits Joe, he wears a feathered cowboy hat and holds his can of beer aloft like the torch atop the Statue of Liberty. With this distinctive pose that welcomed many weary travelers to a land of opportunity, he invites Beverly into his house and back into his life. By incorporating the old sign into a radically new context, Mason suggests that Beverly must redefine her notion of freedom.

Confronted with this ironic depiction of liberty, Beverly temporarily experiences only confusion and paralysis, much as Liz does in "Sorghum." Indeed, Joe's final words to Beverly are a harsh indictment of her failure to make choices. "You're so full of wants you don't know what you want," he says disgustedly (*LL*, 231). In spite of Joe's condemnation, Mason invites us to see Beverly's situation more positively. In an interview with Craig Gholson, she comments:

> Beverly is cutting loose from a marriage that no longer works. It's scary and confusing, and she's not sure what she's going to do or how she's going to make it. But in thinking about this, she's thinking about her parents' world, in which people stayed married whether they liked it or not. And nowadays they don't have to. There's a passage toward the end which has her thinking about how many choices we have these days. . . . it means that she could do something with her life. . . . make it through this chaotic time . . . and get beyond the trap that she was in.[34]

In the story's final paragraphs Beverly appears to be doing just that. She tells herself that working out what she really wants "ought to be so easy" (*LL*, 231). No longer like a stalled car, she embraces the possibilities before her by considering the rhetorical question, "Who knew what might happen or what anybody would decide to do on any given weekend or at any stage of life?" (232).

Beverly's final act is a ritualistic sorting. She goes through the previous day's mail and carefully separates pieces addressed to Joe from those directed to her. At the same time she distinguishes junk mail from items of significance. Finally, she places Joe's mail next to a borrowed videotape she had forgotten but now plans to return to him. Such deliberate actions suggest movement toward closure. In sorting through old mail, Beverly begins to clarify her confused relationship with Joe. In calmly separating his concerns from hers, the trivial from the important, she establishes an appropriate foundation for her future identity. By throwing away junk mail, she counters tendencies toward vacuous excess. By discarding all extraneous parts, she can perhaps begin to put together the pieces of her puzzle. Like so many characters at the conclusions of Mason's stories, Beverly seems on the verge of something. Or, as a more cynical reader might say, she is "on the verge of just being on the verge" (Gholson, 43).

"The Secret of the Pyramids" (1988)

Barbara, the protagonist in "The Secret of the Pyramids," travels from her home in Paducah to Cairo. There she hears an elaborate tale that purportedly reveals the mystery of the ancient pyramids. Ironically, Barbara's destination is not exotic Egypt but the river town of Cairo (pronounced "Karo," like the syrup), Illinois. Her traveling companion is Bob Morganfield, a married man who takes Barbara to an out-of-town restaurant merely to keep their affair secret. Furthermore, the mysterious narrative is little more than a crude joke told by her drunken escort to explain why all young men from western Kentucky make pilgrimages to Cairo. According to Bob's outrageous story, Egyptian explorers paddled their canoes up the Mississippi, discovered a place that reminded them of home, named it Cairo, and proceeded to build pyramids. Later the pyramids collapsed and became infested with snakes, but young men still search among the ruins to discover secrets. Since Bob tells his story in a restaurant that used to be a whorehouse, he is suggesting that young men come to Cairo for sexual initiation.

Bob fabricates his tall tale to entertain and impress Barbara, but this story within a story has greater import. As a parody of the age-old quest narrative, it becomes an ironic commentary on the earnest but largely futile pursuits of Mason's protagonists. Like Beverly's voyages in her imaginary space transporter in "Memphis," the travel story again becomes decidedly mock-heroic. Here the pilgrimage of discovery degenerates into a quick trip for illicit sex. Burning bushes and voices from the clouds provide no dramatic revelations for Bob or Barbara. Just as Cairo, Illinois, is a travesty of the ancient city and Bob's tale is a burlesque, Bob and Barbara's moments of insight are sorely limited. In seeking ultimate truths about life and death, they frequently experience only mock epiphanies.

One such mock epiphany occurs for Bob early one morning near a fountain at the center of the mall where he runs a shoe store. In this unlikely location for revelation, everything looks "fresh and new," like the whole place is "about to bust open like a flower" (*LL,* 74). After seeing a girl in a yellow dress, he experiences "one of those realizations— one of those moments you know you'll remember all your life?" (74). Ironically, Bob's description of this moment of insight is punctuated with a question mark, but he goes on to affirm, "I just suddenly knew where I was and who I was and where I'd always be" (74). After such a comprehensive realization one might expect dramatic action. Bob, however, simply wants to roller-skate through the mall.

In locating Bob's mock epiphany at the center of a shopping mall, Mason makes an apt choice. All across America malls on the outskirts of towns have displaced the towns themselves as centers for commerce and social interaction (especially for teens and the elderly). Malls typically lure crowds with pseudosocial activities like craft exhibits, boat or car shows, and fitness walks. At the same time hard benches and sterile, predictable architecture discourage prolonged lingering. George Lewis notes that "the important thing, from a marketing perspective, is to create the warm *illusion* of community, while at the same time quietly stacking the deck against its development."[35] Both Bob and Barbara work in such a setting, and there Bob experiences an illusion of truth unaccompanied by any real revelation.

Even with the accumulation of ludicrous details surrounding Bob's epiphany, Mason preserves the dignity of her character, but she gently parodies his flash of self-discovery. When Bob describes the episode to Barbara at the restaurant in Cairo, he tries to dramatize the moment by snapping his fingers. Unfortunately, they are so slippery from peeling boiled shrimp that he cannot make a sound. At the peak of Bob's story of enlightenment, the candle on the table flickers out, Bob's face dims, and the darkness prevents the two from reading the dessert menus. Such anticlimactic details suggest that Bob's epiphany is much less dramatic than his inflated account of it.

Although Bob's words and actions are frequently silly, his travel finally assumes greater significance. His automobile takes him not just to the mall and to a gaudy restaurant in Cairo but also to an early death. After his fatal traffic accident Bob can reveal no more secrets, but his sudden death spurs Barbara on to more focused travel.

Barbara ended her affair with Bob in an angry scene that took place several months before his death, but now she must deal with a second distinctive loss. In trying to progress through the various stages of grief and comprehend the mystery of sudden death, Barbara travels to several locations. For Bob the secret of the pyramids that lured boys to Cairo was simply "how to handle women" (*LL*, 73). In Barbara's case the story title has more serious and comprehensive implications. Since the real pyramids were tombs designed to preserve the body for life in another realm, they enclosed the mysteries of death. As one who survives the unexpected death of a lover she thought she hated, Barbara must probe these mysteries. From within the crypt she seeks cryptic knowledge.

In her quest Barbara travels first to the site of Bob's accident. In the middle of the night, she examines shards of glass strewn along the road. In Bob's case superficial stimuli like a mall fountain and a yellow dress triggered a shallow epiphany. For Barbara the stimuli are more intense and the possibilities for insight more profound. As evidence of death and destruction, the shards of glass contrast sharply with the carefully groomed mall, and they suggest the potential for significant revelation. If these fragments contain a secret, however, Barbara is unable to put the pieces back together. The glass shards sparkle in the light from an approaching car, but such a display of brilliance reminds Barbara of nothing more than the rhinestones she glued to her jacket earlier that day.

After a futile trip to the place of Bob's death, she journeys next to the funeral home to view his body. Unfortunately, everything there is calculated to deny glimpses of the truth. The atmosphere of the funeral home approximates the artificiality of the mall in that Bob's body is "lying in the casket like a store display" with flowers arranged "protectively" around it (*LL*, 79). Barbara stares into the face of death but, true to their promise, the morticians have erased all evidence of Bob's accident and fixed "him up like new" (80). A mourner casually remarks, "You can't tell a thing" (80), and this phrase accurately describes the disappointing results of Barbara's quest.

If the pilgrimages in this story are mock-heroic, the rituals surrounding death approximate the burlesque. Ideally this dramaturgy (like any rite of passage) should promote the emotional health of the individual mourner while also affirming the social cohesion of the group. For Barbara, however, the ritual is totally dysfunctional. Since society refuses to acknowledge a dead man's surviving former mistress, she cannot participate in the ceremonies of separation, transition, and incorporation. Robert Fulton describes mourning as "the intersection of grief, a psychological drama, and bereavement, a social drama, where loss through death may find harmonious expression."[36] Denied a part in the larger social drama, Barbara has no opportunity to express her private sorrow and share it with the community.

Even if Barbara could be included in Bob's funeral rituals, the efficacy of those rituals is questionable. Here the mortician's art camouflages death instead of acknowledging it. In such a context "where the everyday reality of dying and bereavement are effectively denied in the first instance," the possibilities for social incorporation of an individual mourner are slight.[37] Jane Littlewood points out that in many contemporary situations death-related rituals "have themselves been removed from the community and have been relocated in the private world of individuals who have been bereaved" (Littlewood, 69). Thus, they may become "rituals of resource management" that "celebrate success in 'doing something about the situation' through rational use of the available resources." Such private rituals help to define the "boundary between the limitations of the past and the prospects for a better future" (Littlewood, 79).

At home after viewing Bob's corpse, Barbara approximates such a ritual by collecting the ephemera of their affair—a balloon from his store, a napkin from a restaurant where they ate, a matchbook and soap from motels they patronized. The many trips in this story have been largely futile, and the story ends with Barbara cataloging various souvenirs of travel. Like the shards of glass, these random fragments from past trips form no coherent pattern, and Barbara apparently intends to destroy them. Poised to do so, she remembers one additional gift from Bob—a guitar-shaped Elvis Presley clock with the 12 letters of Elvis's name substituting for the numbers around the clock face. Instead of discarding this quirky gift, she decides to keep it as a reminder of the fun she shared with Bob and of their "laughter turning to passion" (*LL*, 81). In studying this clock that is "absurd" but nevertheless manages to keep "time perfectly" (81), Barbara finally has a moment of insight and accepts some of life's painful contradictions. Focusing on an embodiment of the ultimate in kitsch, Barbara ironically transcends the mock-heroic.

Leslie White observes that in some of Mason's stories popular culture is a "pervasive stupefying presence" that "wipes out the immediate reality by occupying the space where real engagement might take place."[38] In this particular story, which so often verges on parody, Mason uses an outrageous artifact of popular culture to move her protagonist beyond the trivial and superficial. All around her Barbara finds evidence of ridiculous conjunctions: senior citizens with "CYCLE KILLER" buttons and wrists wrapped in chains stroll around the mall while black limos crowd about the funeral home like dung beetles. When so much of everyday life is bizarre, the hands of an outlandish clock may point the way back to basic truths.

Earlier Barbara denied the grim consequences of time's passage, but now she chooses a timepiece as the most fitting memorial to her dead lover. At the center of this clock is the image of another dead man, Elvis, but as Barbara hangs the clock back on the wall, this figure seems to defy death and "gyrate suggestively" (*LL*, 81). While Elvis dances, the clock hands "read L-V" (81). For the uninitiated such a message might be cryptic, but Barbara can decipher the code and knows that the correct time is 10 past 3. If she has truly probed the secret of the pyramids, she will also realize that this time is not too late for her to get on with her travels through life.

"Drawing Names" (1981)

The word "convention" can refer both to the action of coming together and to a commonly agreed-upon pattern of behavior. In "Drawing Names" an extended family comes together physically, but commonality of values and behavior is elusive. The family's travel to a reunion produces little real unity.

In "Sorghum" Ed Summer comments that a traditional wild-game dinner held each fall is "supposed to mean something" (*LL*, 207), but the event turns out to be shallow and pretentious. "Drawing Names" focuses on an even more important meal—a Christmas dinner that is fraught with high expectations but extremely short on fulfillment. Mason has said that the members of her far-flung family always come home for Christmas and that their elaborate Christmas dinner "defines the family and replenishes us for another year" ("Way," 94). In "Drawing Names" the Sisson family assembles to celebrate the holiday, but (with one character recently divorced and another secretly separated) the story is, in reality, an account of a family falling apart amid the pretense of festivities. At this time of advent, the long-expected guest never arrives; the most extravagantly wrapped gift remains under the tree unopened.

All four of the Sisson daughters have traveled away from the family farm, and they illustrate increasingly radical departures from the old ways. As the wife of a local service-station owner and mother of three, Peggy has stayed closest to her rural roots. She is the one daughter who had a real wedding and who remains "daddy's precious little angel" (*S*, 101). Another daughter, Iris, married a state government employee and moved away to Frankfort. Iris and her husband, Ray, have just separated, but he has agreed to come with her to the family Christmas and for the time being to hide the separation from her parents. In a further departure from the old ways, Carolyn has been divorced for two years and has invited her current lover, Kent Ballard, to join her family for Christmas. The youngest daughter, Laura Jean, lives in St. Louis, studies interior decoration, and is presumably "shacking up" (96) with a textiles salesman named Jim Walsh. Laura Jean brings Jim home to show him off even though he is not welcomed by Mr. Sisson. Physically Jim is a big man, and he represents a degree of nonconformity too expansive for this small house.

Stars have traditionally guided travelers, and the star shining atop a Christmas tree symbolizes a special kind of celestial guidance. Such a star has led all the Sisson daughters home, but the diverse paths they have traveled do not really converge. As an ominous hint that this Christmas will be different from previous ones, Carolyn warns her mother, "Your star's about to fall off" (*S*, 94). Carolyn can easily reposition the silver ornament atop the tree, but she cannot so readily reestablish harmony within her family. Indeed, the disintegration of the Sisson family parallels that of the "broken red plastic reindeer" and "crumbling" Styrofoam snowmen that decorate their "pitiful tree" (102).

With fewer gifts under the tree, Mrs. Sisson observes that "it don't seem like Christmas with drawed names" (*S*, 94). Anthropologists point out that rituals of gift giving and receiving affirm community and that gifts brought back by travelers help them to reintegrate with those who have remained at home. Ordinarily, special wrappings and presentation ceremonies elevate the gift above "the sphere of everyday transactions."[39] When the Sissons draw names, however, chance rather than choice links givers to recipients, and the entire process approximates a marketplace exchange.

Just as the Sissons' gift exchange is perfunctory, their shared meal—presumably another ritual of solidarity—is fractured. Margaret Visser has noted that "feasts the world over are given as celebrations of relationship among the diners, and also as expressions of order, knowledge, competence, sympathy, and consensus at least about important aspects of the value system that supports the group."[40] Despite the abundance of food, most of these intangible elements are absent from the Sissons' feast. It begins without ceremony since no one remembers to ask Pappy to "turn thanks" (*S*, 101). Throughout the meal conversation at the table must compete with noise from the television set, and Carolyn's father eats only a few bites before suddenly leaving the table to watch a football game. Visser describes table manners as ritual movements "to handle the mightiest of necessities, the most potent of symbols, the medium through which we repeatedly express our relationships with each other" (Visser, 4). Conduct at the Sisson table is abrupt and thus indicative of very strained relationships.

Carolyn's mother expects 16 people for this Christmas dinner, but the modest farmhouse is too small for so many guests. Along with the scarcity of physical space is a more critical dearth of emotional space. The old-fashioned, circumscribed values of Carolyn's parents, who have never traveled far from the farm, can hardly accommodate the burgeoning demands for liberation by a later generation.

Carolyn's mother tries to assimilate the geographical and cultural journeys of her four daughters and to adapt as necessary. Like Cleo in "Old Things" and Lila in *Spence + Lila,* she is a seamstress, and an anecdote about sewing illustrates her strategies for coping. When Mrs. Sisson makes a dress for a woman who is extremely obese, she cannot find any pattern that is big enough. After buying the largest one available, she still has "to 'low [i.e., allow] a foot" extra (S, 95) to enclose the woman's girth. Just as the original dress pattern is too restrictive and must be enlarged, the old social patterns require alteration to accommodate changing social conditions and behaviors.

The long-expected guest who never arrives at the Sisson Christmas dinner is Carolyn's lover, Kent. Even after accepting Carolyn's invitation, he spends the day alone at the lake attending to his boat. In choosing an activity that seems sadly out of season, in preferring contact with an object to interaction with humans, Kent reveals his essential coldness. On Christmas Day this waylaid traveler neither gives gifts nor accepts the present Carolyn has wrapped so elegantly.

Although Kent spurns both Carolyn's invitation and her gift, Jim Walsh offers her a surprise present. For Laura Jean, Jim is himself like "a splendid Christmas gift" (*S*, 98), and some of his splendor spills over to relieve Carolyn's gloom. When he sees that Carolyn feels abandoned, he offers words of comfort that are "unexpectedly kind, genuine" (107). As Jim smiles broadly, she sees inside his mouth "a gold cap on a molar, shining like a Christmas ornament" (107). In this unusual location Carolyn has finally discovered an untarnished emblem of Christmas. Although Jim is an outsider hardly welcome at the Sisson family Christmas, he becomes for Carolyn an embodiment of the true Christmas spirit. Karen Underwood (in a somewhat strained reading of this story) has even compared Jim to Balthazar, one of the three Magi in the story of Christ's nativity.[41] Like this king, Jim travels far to bring a very special gift. Jim's candor reveals inner gold, and his obvious love for Laura Jean provides for Carolyn hope that her own future will be more joyous. Carolyn cannot repair all the rifts in her extended family, but as a traveler who has just discovered a new and unusual guiding star, she can chart a new direction for herself.

Like other female protagonists in "Sorghum," "Memphis," and "The Secret of the Pyramids," Carolyn is ready to embark on a journey that is hardly traditional for women. Carolyn Heilbrun has noted that "in literature and out, through all recorded history, women have lived by a script they did not write." In this prescribed plot their role was largely passive and static—"to be given by one man, the father, to another, the husband; to become the mother of men."[42] In this story of falling stars and confused gift giving, Carolyn moves beyond the established courtship and marriage plot and pursues a dynamic role in a new script. She and other Mason heroines are ready to act out the quest plot—one heretofore largely reserved for men. As a traditional wife and seamstress, Carolyn's mother replays the role of Penelope, who patiently sewed and awaited the return of her adventurer husband. Carolyn, on the other hand, spurns the needle and aspires to become the adventurer.

"Detroit Skyline, 1949" (1981)

Among Mason's collected stories, "Detroit Skyline, 1949" is an anomaly. Mason's settings are usually Southern and contemporary but, as the title implies, the setting here is the industrial North several decades earlier. More commonly Mason's characters are adults experiencing midlife crises like divorce or senior citizens confronting retirement or debilitating illness. The central character in "Detroit Skyline, 1949" is a nine-year-old girl about to emerge from childhood into adolescence. Mason uses first-person narration infrequently, but here this point of view allows a revealing double perspective. It displays firsthand the naive behavior of the child, but, since time has elapsed and the narrator is now more mature, it also permits bemused detachment.

Mason has commented that this travel story was motivated by her faint recollection of a trip she took with her mother as a child. On that trip from rural Kentucky to the home of relatives near Detroit, Mason "was captivated by the television set, and the story was originally called 'The Television Set.' " Because her memories of the summer of 1949 were fuzzy, Mason read "two weeks worth of microfilm of the *Detroit Free Press*" and discovered stories about polio epidemics, the city bus strike, and the pervasive Communist scare. Then she "invented the story about the mother's miscarriage" and worked all these strands into her narrative.[43] With these enriching additions the story became much more than an account of a young girl's first exposure to television.

According to the taxonomy suggested by Mordecai Marcus, "Detroit Skyline, 1949" is a tentative initiation story. It brings the protagonist to a threshold of understanding and maturity but does not allow her to cross.[44] Although Peggy Jo's rite of passage remains incomplete, the story includes many motifs typical of initiation stories. One common initiation pattern restricts the protagonist to a limited, familiar environ-ment but subverts innocence by introducing an interloper representa-tive of the larger world. Such is the case for Seth in Robert Penn War-ren's "Blackberry Winter" and for Sylvia in Sarah Orne Jewett's "A White Heron." In keeping with her emphasis on travelers and pilgrims, Mason chooses an inverse but equally common pattern of initiation. Peggy's primary action is a journey from the country to the city—from the safely familiar to the mysteriously ominous. She travels with a mature guide, her mother, but this guide is not always able to protect her from hurt or answer troubling questions. As in many initiation stories Peggy con-fronts the mysteries of adult sexuality, sickness, and death. Because she is only nine, however, such confrontations usually leave her more bewil-dered than enlightened. Indeed, Peggy is the same age as Sylvia in "A White Heron" and Seth in "Blackberry Winter," and like these two char-acters she is frequently puzzled by intimations of mortality all around her.

In traveling to Detroit, Peggy follows the path of relatives who have left the more innocent agrarian South for jobs in the industrial North. Such migrations are not entirely successful, and thus they foreshadow the incompleteness of Peggy's passage. Her Uncle Boone now works in an automobile factory and has acquired a comfortable house. Instead of finding himself, however, he leads a decidedly fragmented life. He can never build a complete car because all he knows is bumpers. Unable to afford the automobiles he helps to assemble, Boone is left stranded by a public bus strike. Boone Cashon's two names (one the surname of a famous pioneer and the other an echo of the cliché "cash on the barrelhead") probably suggest a conflict between his frontier heritage and the crass world where he now works.

A further suggestion of separation from and nostalgic longing for the agrarian ideal surfaces in the reading material of Boone's daughter, Betsy Lou. Surrounded by the factories of Detroit, she reads Louis Bromfield's *Pleasant Valley*. This idyllic account of Malabar Farm, established in rural Ohio in 1939, is far removed from her urban life, and the allusion suggests another failed or sharply truncated journey. Betsy Lou can hardly realize Bromfield's pastoral vision, just as Peggy will not complete her journey of initiation.

Many initiation stories move from darkness to light—from symbolic sleep to harsh awakening. Accordingly, after an all-night bus trip Peggy steps off into a Detroit suburb and wakes up to a strange and confusing world. Here, if she leaves the house of Aunt Mozelle and Uncle Boone, she risks being stricken with polio. Even within the house she reads in her aunt's scrapbooks about bizarre occurrences such as kidnappings, diseases, and disasters all around the world. Peggy's teenaged cousin, Betsy Lou, has three dates in one day, and these mature courting practices mystify Peggy. Lunetta, an unmarried friend of Mozelle's, introduces more bizarre hints of adult sexuality. Her elaborate costumes and thick lipstick function as "man bait" (*S*, 41), and she tells complicated stories about adulterous relationships. All the adults around Peggy discuss Communist infiltration of labor unions and the danger that any worker who even knows a Communist will be fired. In Peggy's new environment even playtime is frightening. Sharon Belletieri, a new playmate from down the street, zooms along the sidewalk on her roller skates and laughs at Peggy's clumsiness. Peggy has never skated before and has as much difficulty keeping her physical balance as she does maintaining her psychological equilibrium.

In several other scenes Peggy's physical acts objectify her confusion. At a children's birthday party, for example, the game of pin the tail on the donkey becomes a dramatic enactment of her inner state. Immediately after Sharon has neatly pinned a label on Uncle Boone's coworker by asserting that he is a Communist, Peggy finds herself blindfolded and being spun in circles. She becomes dizzy and attaches the donkey tail to a flower on the wallpaper instead of to the elusive animal. Peggy's blindness and disorientation in the game are comparable to her intellectual and emotional confusion in this strange new world.

Just as Peggy's eyes fail her in the party game, her powers of speech and aural comprehension frequently prove deficient to meet the challenges of her new environment. In a realm where people speak a new or coded language, the initiate is sometimes both deaf and dumb. Peggy's speech is that of the rural South, and her playmate Sharon cannot understand her pronunciation of simple words like "hair." On the other hand, when Sharon says Peggy's name it comes out sounding like "piggy." Peggy cannot communicate easily even with her own cousin. To Betsy Lou's greeting of "Hey," Peggy responds timidly with "Corn." This country joke bewilders Betsy Lou, and she stares at Peggy as though she were "some odd sort of pet allowed into the house" (*S*, 36). Such verbal misunderstandings provide incidental humor, but they also reinforce the story's major theme. In her initiation Peggy must expand her vocabulary and absorb new idioms as mechanisms for ordering this strange new world. Her adult relatives expose her to unfamiliar words like "reds" but offer no clarification of the code. In fact, the adults proclaim that such terms "don't concern younguns" (43). Scorned by the neighborhood children because she doesn't speak or comprehend their language, Peggy is not yet accepted into adult conversation. She knows the terms appropriate to this discourse but does not understand their signification.

The decisive event in Peggy's rite of passage is her mother's miscarriage. Already puzzled by earlier events and unable to understand the adult talk she overhears, Peggy becomes terrified. Peggy's mother miscarries without even knowing she was pregnant, and this totally unexpected development makes her role as mother and guide especially difficult. Like Nick Adams's father in the Hemingway story "Indian Camp," she must clarify for her child the mysteries of life's beginning as well as its ending. The complicated circumstances force her to explain how the potential for birth has been abruptly displaced by the reality of death. In her attempt she first tells Peggy that she was going to have a baby brother or sister. Then she hastily retracts and says, "I'm trying to tell you there wasn't really a baby. I didn't know about it, anyway" (*S*, 49). Retreating to a rural analogy (suggesting perhaps the lost order and simplicity of an agrarian culture), she compares her situation to that of a hen that failed to hatch some of its eggs. Throughout this halting conversation Peggy's mother seems as confused about proper idioms as Peggy. Even if she understands the coded discourse of adults, she cannot share it with her daughter.

With its disturbing conjunction of sexuality and mortality, this scene recalls one of the Miranda stories by Katherine Anne Porter. In "The Grave" another nine-year-old girl must face the mysteries of birth and death as she examines the body of a dead rabbit with babies in its womb almost ready to be born. These fetal rabbits are obscured by a thin red veil (presumably the amniotic sac), but in her struggle toward mature awareness Miranda wants desperately to break through this symbolic veil so she can see and know all. Since this action takes place in an abandoned cemetery, the echoes of mortality become even more strident.

Just as Peggy's mother's pregnancy and that of the rabbit in "The Grave" are abortive, Peggy's initiation is incomplete. Her journey is supposed to take her from the farm to the big city, but, in fact, she never gets close enough to see even the skyline of Detroit. Peggy merely glimpses the tall buildings on a television newscast, and there she sees only "some faint, dark shapes, hiding behind the snow, like a forest in winter" (*S*, 50). The television (literally, vision from afar) provides a semblance of truth but obscures more than it reveals. Thus, Peggy's exposure to the big city is indirect just as her experience of the story's sharpest pain—her mother's miscarriage—is vicarious. Like the mysteries of life in "The Grave," the city remains hidden behind a veil.

In her room alone after watching the fuzzy television newscast, Peggy experiences a vision of truth in which she claims to see "everything clearly" (*S*, 50). This vision (much like Bob's mock epiphany in "The Secret of the Pyramids") presumably explains all the mysteries of her time away from home: "My mother had said an egg didn't hatch, but I knew better. The reds had stolen the baby. They took things. They were after my aunt's copper-bottomed pans. . . . They wanted my uncle's job. They were invisible . . . although they might wear disguises. You didn't know who might be a red. You never knew when you might lose a baby that you didn't know you had. I understood it all" (50). These musings of a precocious nine-year-old are both charmingly naive and brilliantly insightful. Because Peggy cannot understand the adult codes, she obviously has facts garbled, but her assertions capture important truths. Although the specific labels she assigns to the forces of evil may be erroneous, she is correct in perceiving that it can be both immanent and imminent. Since she cannot escape its influence, she must be prepared at any moment.

Although Peggy's initiation is incomplete, the journey does change her profoundly. She returns to Kentucky with an acute appreciation of "the mystery of travel, the vastness of the world, the strangeness of life" (*S*, 51). The bus drops Peggy and her mother at an intersection half a mile from their home. As they walk toward the farm, Peggy sees their white house and tin-roofed barn amid tall oak trees. In the final sentence of the story, however, this Kentucky skyline is still in the distance. Just as Peggy never traveled all the way to Detroit, the story ends without her ever returning all the way home. Having experienced so much that was new, Peggy cannot easily return to her old self and remains in limbo.

"State Champions" (1987)

Both "Detroit Skyline, 1949" and "State Champions" focus on a girl named Peggy who experiences problems of growing up. In the earlier story the main character is 9 years old, and in the sequel (set 3 years later in 1952) she is 12. Mason's sequel continues a major theme introduced in the earlier story. During her trip to the suburbs of Detroit, the younger Peggy confronts mysteries of adult sexuality and death but returns home to Kentucky more confused than enlightened. In "State Champions" the slightly older Peggy remains in rural Kentucky but moves significantly further along the path of initiation. She does not embark on another physical trip, but she does travel metaphorically and vicariously.

As a seventh grader Peggy learns rapidly about sex. When a male student shows Peggy a pornographic comic, she is both disgusted and thrilled. Later she learns that the older sister of a classmate is pregnant and will soon marry her boyfriend and drop out of school. Indeed, Peggy knows that classes at her school shrink dramatically as students leave to have babies. They seem simply to disappear like "calves going off to the slaughterhouse in the fall" (*LL*, 141), and such a fatalistic image suggests Peggy's own impending loss of innocence. As in "Detroit Skyline, 1949" this metaphor links sexuality to mortality and again conjoins two central mysteries of growing up.

The specter of teen pregnancy is ominous but not as daunting to Peggy as her brushes with illness and death. On an overnight visit she meets a friend's invalid grandmother. This old woman is confined to a wheelchair and unable to speak, but throughout the cold night she squeaks plaintively like a mouse. Back at school Peggy hears about the death of another friend's sister in an automobile accident. As the classroom door opens, Peggy expects a student with homemade candy to sell rather than a grim announcement of death. Ironically, she is "hoping for divinity" (*LL*, 142) but gets instead the harsh shock of mortality. Leslie Fiedler has described the initiation journey as "a fall through knowledge to maturity." Always in the background "there persists the myth of the

Garden of Eden, the assumption that to know good and evil is to be done with the joy of innocence and to take on the burdens of work and childbearing and death."[45] For Peggy such knowledge remains incomplete, but its intimations are becoming increasingly more insistent.

The 12-year-old girl in "State Champions" is certainly more worldly wise than the 9-year-old in "Detroit Skyline, 1949," but she is still puzzled by her new experiences. As in the earlier story Peggy does not fully comprehend the prevailing communication codes. On the playground her boyfriend offers to teach her sexually suggestive hand signals, but she thinks he has in mind the signals used by drivers to indicate turns. Peggy soon recognizes the danger of being uninitiated. If she cannot decode the signal of a boy's index finger lightly scraping her palm, she may respond incorrectly and "inadvertently agree to do something" that she had "no intention of doing" (*LL*, 139).

Even if Peggy is the protagonist of this story, she does not get top billing in its title. While Peggy herself remains confined to her rural home and provincial school, the basketball team from tiny Cuba, Kentucky, is a vanguard that storms and conquers the larger world. These farm boys who practice out behind the barn manage to travel afar and defeat a strong team from the big city of Louisville. While "Detroit Skyline, 1949" emphasized play (e.g., skating and pinning the tail on the donkey), this story progresses to sports—institutionalized competition for an extrinsic prize. Such a progression parallels Peggy's gradual movement from childish to more adult concerns. Nevertheless, the champion basketball players (including Peggy's boyfriend Glenn) are known as the Cubs, and this juvenile nickname supports Mason's theme of incomplete initiation. Despite their victories the boys from Cuba are still callow and immature. Left behind to listen to the tournament games on the radio, Peggy is even younger and more inexperienced than these big high school boys.

Social theorists working in the functionalist tradition of Emile Durkheim have likened sporting events to sacred ceremonies and sports teams to totemic embodiments of a larger community's identity. Indeed, sporting events are typically set apart from profane daily life by elaborate vestments (team uniforms), rituals (prescribed opening ceremonies, formal handshakes or bows to opponents, ordered progressions through set patterns of innings, quarters, etc.), and taboos (unambiguous rules enforced by umpires or referees). In their trip to the state tournament, the Cuba Cubs maneuver up and down the standard hardwood floor, but in doing so they also explore the sacred mysteries of a strange new realm. Although Peggy does not participate directly in such ceremonies, the stellar achievement of the totemic team provides her with a vicarious taste of achievement in the world beyond insular Cuba. The triumphant players return from the tournament in Lexington like pilgrims from the Holy Land, like knights who have sought and won the Holy Grail. Accordingly, fans meet them at the bridge over Kentucky Lake and escort them home. As a concrete boundary between Peggy's rural environment and the exciting larger world, the bridge indicates the limits of her present development. She has not yet crossed this symbolic bridge but will no doubt do so in the future. In their success as travelers, the basketball team provides a pattern for her to emulate. Exactly what Peggy aspires to do in later life remains unclear even to her, but many details indicate that she will surely travel beyond the limitations of Cuba—that she will use her abilities in creating something more than a baby.

At the end of "Shiloh," Norma Jean stands on the west bank of the Tennessee River looking out over the water to the other side. She does not yet see the best way to reach the next stage in her life, but her gaze is focused intently on it. Peggy in "State Champions" is not actually poised on the riverbank, but she has metaphorically been to the bridge and glimpsed the glories beyond that river.

"The Ocean" (1981)

At the beginning of "The Ocean," Imogene and Bill Crittendon drive down the highway in their RV and yell out to a perfect stranger, "Which way's 65!" (*S*, 148). In the immediate context this question is a request for directions to the interstate highway leading south to Florida. In a larger sense it is a plea for help in charting the proper course (past the crucial age of 65) to a peaceful retirement—a journey much different from that in "Detroit Skyline, 1949" and "State Champions." The Crittendons have just sold their cows and farm, given their household goods to their children, and set out to see the world in their new camper cruiser. They think retirement should allow them to "start all over again" (151), but this new beginning is elusive. They have been "tied down on a farm all this time" (158), and when these moorings are cut they find themselves hopelessly adrift.

The ocean in Mason's title refers specifically to the Crittendons' destination along the east coast of Florida, but it also becomes a metaphor for their confusion in the journey through life. Like an ocean the interstate highway seems "to go on forever" and has mirages shining "like whitecaps" in the distance (*S*, 148). In this figurative transformation of road to body of water, Mason emphasizes the Crittendons' difficulty in navigating. Since the ocean has no clearly marked paths, sea travelers (and retirees) must define their own routes. In the vast expanse of water, they can easily become confused and perhaps even swamped by the waves. Like the elderly people in Stanley Ellin's "The Blessington Method," the Crittendons are no longer either producers or consumers. Aboard their RV cruiser (their last major purchase) and now largely superfluous to society, they become little more than flotsam on strange waters.

Several other images display the Crittendons' bewilderment in their new stage of life. In saying they "blazed a trail to Nashville" (*S*, 148), Mason implies that in retirement they have had to travel like pioneers through an unmarked wilderness. Along a secondary road in Georgia, Bill tries to read a fading Burma-Shave sign, but because one word is missing the remainder is incoherent. Bill tries to decipher this enigmatic message from the past as if it might contain some wisdom for the future, but in doing so he almost wrecks the camper.

Although this story about older people has few trendy references to popular culture, Mason does use several details from current events as indirect commentary on the Crittendons' situation. Their former life on the farm was cohesive, with their well-established connections to the community and the land. Having sold their farm and left old friends behind, Bill and Imogene have severed important ties. When Bill comments on a new treaty between the United States and Panama, Mason suggests an analogy with his own situation. According to Bill, the Atlantic Ocean was securely connected to the Pacific until President Carter gave away the canal, but now that crucial linkage is broken. Bill is equally upset with Carter's decision "to be buddies with the Communists" in China (*S*, 152) and to abandon the true Chinese government in Taiwan. Like the Taiwanese, he and Imogene are exiles far from home. The breach in relations between Taiwan and the United States is analogous to their break with the past.

In international diplomacy as well as in individual lives, integrating past history with present practice is a difficult task. Obviously, the RV does not allow the Crittendons to bring along much of their past, but the resonance of things left behind is haunting. Bill misses his dog and, even though his cows are gone, he still gets up at four because that is milking time. In another recent story about an elderly traveler, James

Fetler's "The Dust of Yuri Serafimovich," the protagonist maintains a faithful if tenuous attachment to his native city. Through years of wandering all over the globe, he always carries with him a bucket of soil from home. Continued connection to a beloved place can provide solace and stability as one grows old, but in their cramped RV the Crittendons have not so much as a cupful of Kentucky dirt to sustain them.

Bill hopes to resolve his problems by completing his pilgrimage and seeing the ocean once more. He attaches so much importance to the ocean because it recalls for him his youthful days in the navy during World War II. There (like the navy veteran Spence in *Spence + Lila*) he was surrounded by danger but came away safe and whole. In journeying to Florida, where earlier explorers sought the fountain of youth, he seeks a return to that youthful state of freedom and excitement. When he finally looks out over the surf, he tells himself that it is "the same water, carried around by time, that he had sailed" years ago (S, 164). Growing old and cut off from his past, Bill desperately needs this assurance of continuity. Unfortunately, the end of the story suggests that Bill's quest is a failure. On the horizon he sees destroyers and battleships—omens of strife rather than peace—and he is unable to decide if they are "coming or going, or whose they" are (164). At the end of his highway, Bill has lost his sense of direction and cannot distinguish friend from foe.

Along the route to Florida, Bill makes friends with several dogs in campgrounds. One dog to which he takes a special liking has the distinctive name Ishmael. By giving the dog this inauspicious name, Mason links Bill with a long tradition of outcasts and wanderers. In spite of navigational difficulties, Bill and Imogene do reach the ocean, but this destination fails to provide the peace and comfort they sought. Their only recourse is to climb back into the RV and wander along other routes. Mason's original title for this story was "Recreation," and this name suggests an ominous pun.[46] In their retirement the Crittendons seek a life of refreshing leisure. Instead, they must move along and continually try to reconstruct their disconnected lives. Cut off from the past, they must forge new connections at each stop. Despite its name the fancy *recreational* vehicle is an inadequate instrument for this task of repeated creation. Like Beverly's "sunshine coffin" in "Memphis," it is only a fantasy transporter.

In her treatment of elderly travelers in "The Ocean," Mason has diverted the traditional American travel story from its typical course. This is Mason's only story set exclusively on the open road, but instead of exulting in the promise of an endless highway, it mourns the loss of stability and permanence. This bumpy detour from established American mythology ends on the Atlantic coast rather than on the glorious Western frontier. Such an itinerary suggests a need for reexamining old values, retracing familiar routes in the cultural landscape. Several of Mason's other stories display such recursive travel by protagonists who have ventured far away geographically and culturally. As they return to their rural homes, they scrutinize local culture from the perspective of outsiders and attempt to harmonize their own divergent experiences.

"Nancy Culpepper" (1981)

One of Mason's best examinations of recursive travel is the story "Nancy Culpepper." Here the eponymous heroine has journeyed far away from her Kentucky home and has lived for many years in other parts of the country. In returning to the farm to visit her invalid grandmother, she again embraces the local while maintaining her allegiance to the remote.

As in "Detroit Skyline, 1949" and "The Ocean," physical travel by characters in this story correlates closely with significant passages—transitions from one stage of life to the next or from one culture to another. Among the most critical transitions in the past was Nancy's travel from adolescence to maturity—her move from Kentucky to the Northeast and her subsequent marriage to Jack Cleveland, a native of that area. The current transition, which motivates much of the story's action, is the impending move to a nursing home by Nancy's 93-year-old grandmother. A major transition that may occur in the not-so-distant future is Nancy's move back to Kentucky with her photographer husband and young son.

As a narrative technique for examining these difficult passages in time and place, Mason uses vivid flashbacks. To create an evocative pattern of imagery that reinforces this narrative technique, she includes many references to photography. Such images are apt because the eye of the camera can probe both the temporal and the spatial dimensions of reality, permitting an illusion of travel to former times and distant places. Of this manipulation in two dimensions, Susan Sontag writes: "Photographs are a way of imprisoning reality, understood as recalcitrant, inaccessible; of making it stand still. Or they enlarge a reality that is felt to be shrunk, hollowed out, perishable, remote."[47] A still photograph presumably stops time, and Nancy goes home to Kentucky to keep her grandmother's family pictures from getting lost in the move.

She wants to save Granny's pictures as souvenirs and thus preserve spots of time long past. Jack Cleveland's contemporary photographs pose significant questions about spatial relationships. His "bizarre still lifes with light bulbs, wine bottles, Tinker Toys, [and] Lucite cubes" (*S*, 185) bring apparently unrelated objects into an odd union. Such oddities of photographic composition parallel the accidents of travel that have brought together people as different as Nancy and Jack.

Nancy's marriage to Jack may be like an unusual photographic composition, but another photographic metaphor used to examine this transition is even more incisive. Mason notes that most of the Cleveland wedding pictures "turned out to be trick photography—blurred faces and double exposures" (*S*, 181). This metaphor suggests that Nancy's marriage to Jack is not just an odd juxtaposition. Like the wedding pictures, it is actually a superimposition of one culture over another. In such a palimpsest, present actions may obscure past values, but both are vital parts of the total picture.

Specific details of the wedding, described in a lengthy flashback, provide abundant evidence of this superimposition. Nancy has been living with Jack for almost a year and does not want her parents to travel north to join them for the 10-minute ceremony. Despite her own long journey away from home and the absence of her family, Nancy has not completely abandoned the cultural values of rural Kentucky. As she says her vows, she is shocked by the bearded, chain-smoking minister and remembers preachers from her childhood who would have labeled him a heathen. Nancy and Jack are "lone travelers on the edge of some outer-space adventure" (*S*, 181), but she remains preoccupied with memories that are decidedly local—country food and blackberry bushes on the Kentucky farm.

Any photograph that truly captures Nancy's condition on her wedding day will have to be blurred or doubly exposed. Her physical travels have been extensive and swift, and her mental activity is so kinetic that even the fastest shutter speed cannot stop the motion. In this transition from one place to another, from old family to new, her confused sense of identity is analogous to an overlay where one image competes for attention with another.

If the double exposure is an apt metaphor for Nancy Culpepper's transition to Nancy Cleveland, Mason uses another kind of photograph to examine the passage Granny must undergo as she travels to the nursing home. Instead of looking at pictures from recent times, Granny (with help from Nancy) studies brownish photographs from the past.

These images are "sharp and clear" (*S*, 194), but, to accommodate the primitive cameras, poses were stiff. Such rigid postures prevented blurring and hence stopped time, but they now seem highly artificial.

Granny's problem is that her present actions imitate the rigidity of old photographs. Even though she is crippled with arthritis and confined to her bed, she stubbornly resists moving on to Orchard Acres Rest Home, and her fear of this trip reflects a more general resistance to change. Set in the ways of the past, she insists that her dishes be washed with old-fashioned lye soap. Even though her children can no longer care for her because of their own health problems, she remains (like the pose in an old picture) "dead set" against going to the nursing home (*S*, 191).

Granny acts out this stubborn resistance to change as she examines a picture of herself as a girl. "That's me," she asserts (*S*, 193), as if an emphatic use of present tense could obliterate intervening years. When Nancy fails to see the resemblance, Granny proclaims, "Why, it looks just *like* me," and "strokes the picture, as though she were trying to feel the dress" (193). Such action reflects a naive view of photography that makes little distinction between the thing photographed and its image. Primitive societies view the subject and its representation simply as two different but closely related manifestations of one spirit. In this case, however, neither Granny's verbal decree nor her ritualistic manipulation of the photograph provides a return to youth or talismanic resurgence of power.

Nancy also searches among Granny's old pictures for a photograph of her namesake—the Nancy Culpepper who lived several generations earlier. By studying a fixed image from the past, Nancy hopes to resolve her own blurred identity. These efforts fail, however, because the photographs are not labeled, and none can be unequivocally identified as Nancy Culpepper. As G. O. Morphew observes, "the confusion surrounding the identity of the original Nancy perfectly reflects the confusion of identity of the contemporary Nancy."[48]

As an oblique commentary on Nancy's futile effort to travel into the past, Mason introduces still another photographic image. Nancy first learned about her same-name ancestor when she took her grandmother to the Culpepper graveyard some years earlier. On this trip Nancy saw a tombstone marked "NANCY CULPEPPER, 1833–1905" and "did a double take" (*S*, 186). Later she compares the experience to "time-lapse photography" that enables her to look "into the past and the future at the same time" (186–87). In contrast to other references to pictures, this image of a time-lapse photograph suggests a more appropriate way of viewing life's transitions and coping with the stresses of rapid travels through space and time. The antique photographs in the story are static and frequently emblematic of refusal to change with the times. The doubly exposed pictures of Nancy's wedding exhibit competing images and discontinuity of past and present. On the other hand, a time-lapse photograph displays no sharp image, but it does show a definite progression—a clear path of transition. Instead of stopping time, it records steady movement through time.

In revealing not an object but a path, the time-lapse photograph provides a valuable lesson in charting life's passages. It shows the need to stress fluidity rather than static identity. As Nancy dances with Jack at her wedding, she laments, "There aren't any stopping places. . . . Songs used to have stopping places in between" (*S*, 182). In the dance of life, Nancy cannot stop to find herself in a photograph from the past but must embrace the ongoing processes of living. In traveling away from Kentucky or back again, she must focus on recursive action rather than destination, on integration rather than distinction.

"Lying Doggo" (1982)

Even though Mason sets several of her works in the fictional town of Hopewell, Kentucky, the same characters seldom appear in more than one of her stories. The main characters in "Nancy Culpepper" are notable exceptions. Nancy, her husband, Jack, and their son, Robert, develop further in the story "Lying Doggo." In a later work, the short novel *Spence + Lila*, the recursive traveler Nancy appears back home again with her parents, and this time (approximately five years later) we also learn about her brother, sister, nieces, and nephews.

The immediate action of "Lying Doggo" involves little travel, but Nancy does recall extensive wanderings both with and without Jack before they settled in Pennsylvania. Furthermore, since "Lying Doggo" appears immediately after "Nancy Culpepper" in the *Shiloh* collection and continues the theme of painful transitions, discussion of this sequel is appropriate here. One year has elapsed since the time of "Nancy Culpepper," Robert is now a very precocious nine-year-old, and Granny has died. (News of Granny's death reached Nancy while she was on still another trip in the as yet uncollected story "Blue Country.") Rather than focusing on Granny, however, this story deals with the family dog, Grover Cleveland. Like Granny he is racked with arthritis, and his own death is imminent.

The story's title is a colloquial phrase that means lying in hiding. This title refers specifically to Grover's lying before the fire in a state of complete immobility that makes it difficult to determine whether he is alive or dead. At the same time the phrase suggests other troubles that may lie in hiding to ambush an unsuspecting traveler. Within the story such troubles include portentous passages—loss of innocence for Robert, possible problems in Nancy and Jack's marriage, and the outbreak of potentially fatal hepatitis at the school where Nancy is principal.

"Lying Doggo" examines a dimension of the travel theme very different from that in "Midnight Magic." In "Midnight Magic" the central emblem is a fast car that is sometimes compared to a panting dog, but here the most significant image is an animal whose crippled legs make him barely able to move at all. "Midnight Magic" displays the allure of movement—to any place at any time—for a character who is immature and unenlightened. "Lying Doggo" focuses on older characters who have traveled as hippies all over the country accompanied by the dog, Grover. Now that Grover's mobility is so severely limited, his condition forces Nancy and Jack to reflect on their own passages through life. A vivid reminder of past ramblings, Grover is also a portent of changes to come. In contemplating Grover, Nancy and Jack relive their wandering days and mediate the uneasy boundary between stability and flux.

In dealing with the invalid dog, the Cleveland family must decide when to let go of their pet and their collective past. Nancy hopes "he can hang on" (*S*, 206) as long as they assist him with basic body functions and confesses that she is like her Granny who "just clung to life, long after her body was ready to die" (202). Jack, however, insists that he doesn't "want to cling to the past" (208) and argues that it is time to have Grover put to sleep.

The Cleveland family name suggests a pun that characterizes this dilemma of holding on or letting go. Coming from two different roots, the verb "to cleave" has contradictory meanings. In one sense it means to sever or divide by a blow, but it can also mean to adhere or cling to. These divergent meanings illustrate two different responses to change, and the verb's ambiguity parallels the difficulty in deciding which response is appropriate. In language and in the journey of life, the proper choice must depend on context.

In her particular context, Nancy first resists putting Grover to sleep because she feels that Grover's death will mark a milestone in her marriage—a marriage that has survived 15 years and many trips across the country. During several periods when Jack traveled without her, Grover was also absent, and she has an irrational fear "that when the dog is gone, Jack will be gone too" (*S*, 198). During one of these separations, Nancy lived one mile from the San Andreas fault—an intimation that the fault lines in her marriage were as perilous and unpredictable as those of the earth.

To Jack his dog is almost like a child, but he understands the need for proper balance between cleaving to and cleaving in two. For him also the death of Grover is a significant milestone, because in the past rock heroes were the only people whose deaths ever affected him. After the assassination of John Lennon, for example, he and Nancy cried together and acknowledged "that they had lost their youth" (*S*, 201). Now, at a farewell party for the dog, marking also a significant passage in his own life, he raises his glass and offers a calmly acquiescent toast: "Way to go, Grover!" (212).

As in "Nancy Culpepper" brief references to photography again suggest an appropriate response to mutability and death. For Jack a still photograph is not a way to defy change but a graphic reminder of life's impermanence. In his pictures he sees not people or objects but illusions. As an artist he deliberately tries to display "the vulnerability of the image"—an image "meant to evoke its own death" (*S*, 210). For Jack, then, a photograph becomes a memento mori that, as an object of contemplation, may gradually inure one to life's inevitable passages. Susan Sontag asserts that photography is inherently elegiac. "To take a photograph," she says, "is to participate in another person's (or thing's) mortality, vulnerability, mutability. Precisely by slicing out this moment and freezing it, all photographs testify to time's relentless melt" (Sontag, 15). At the beginning of this story, as Jack works in his studio, he sees Grover's face gradually appear on a print in the developing fluid. Just as Grover's face emerges from an apparent void, Grover himself fades quietly away as the story ends, and both events exhibit life's mysterious flux.

As a travel story "Lying Doggo" offers much reflection on past journeys. As an artist, however, Jack anticipates another group of Mason characters. His ordered vision briefly suggests a way of creating meaning out of chaos when that meaning has not been found on the road.

"Residents and Transients" (1982)

"Residents and Transients" focuses on Mary, a somewhat jaded traveler who returns home to enjoy a brief interlude of pastoral calm. In this case home is an old but stately farmhouse in the middle of a cornfield. Mary lives alone on the farm abandoned by her elderly parents when they moved to Florida, eats vegetables grown and canned by her mother, and cares for eight cats. Meanwhile, the call to further travel remains strident. Mary's husband, Stephen, has taken a new job in Louisville and is there hunting for a tract house suitable for them. Mary remains attached to Stephen but is reluctant to leave her childhood home and the hometown lover with whom she is having a brief affair.

The straightforward title of "Residents and Transients" frames a topic for debate. Mason has commented that "Residents and Transients" is a "focal point for the main theme" in her first collection—the tension "between hanging onto the past and racing toward the future." The story shows that some people "would just never leave home, because that's where they're meant to be," while others are (as the Springsteen song proclaims) "born to run" (Wendy Smith, 425).

Mary tries to clarify her position on the value of such travel by considering two kinds of cat populations—those that establish fixed territories and those that roam widely. According to old scientific beliefs, territorial cats were the strongest and most successful whereas transients were losers and bums. Now, however, some researchers claim that transients are superior because they exhibit greater intelligence and heightened curiosity. Because even the experts can't decide, this scientific approach is of little help to Mary.

To further complicate the debate, the story shows that in the human population the dichotomy between residents and transients is not so simple. In fact, significant variations exist within both categories. Some residents, for example, are committed to home only because of ignorance or fear of the unknown. These provincials "would rather die than leave town" (*S*, 122), and they make disparaging remarks when they see outsiders invading their domain. Although this sort of allegiance to home (and aversion to travel) is petty and shallow, other residents have satisfied their curiosity about the outside world and by going far away learned the true value of the place left behind. Some years earlier Mary herself "couldn't wait to get out" (124), but she now wonders why she "ever went away" (121). Like Stephen Dedalus, who leaves Ireland at the end of *A Portrait of the Artist as a Young Man*, Mary eventually learns that the shortest way home may be through a strange land. As a first-person narrator she sometimes pokes fun at her own slowness in appreciating home. She says she was away for eight years "pursuing higher learning" (121). Such stilted phrasing suggests a bemused disdain for chasing after elevated truths when the most basic ones were readily apparent right there at home.

Although becoming a transient for eight years actually made Mary a more enlightened and committed resident, some transients never gain such wisdom. Stephen, for example, has a job that requires constant transfers, and he ranges widely selling word processors with memory. Ironically, he retains no significant memories of where he has been or where he belongs. Instead of discovering any sense of place, he wanders over the land through endless interchangeable pseudoplaces.[49]

Although Stephen has never really resided anywhere, transients of another variety once had a strong sense of place but have now been forced to surrender it. Because of age and illness, Mary's parents left their farmhouse for Florida and now live in an oxymoronic mobile home. Mary's mother valued her real home so highly that she couldn't bear to preside over its dismemberment. She simply departed as if going to shop and left Mary to handle the sorting and sale of her household goods.

Although Mason's stories contain numerous references to popular culture, her allusions to canonical literature are much less frequent. In this story, however, the well-educated narrator flies in a small plane over the fields around her house, and this experience reminds her of "the Dylan Thomas poem with the dream about the birds flying along with the stacks of hay" (*S*, 127). The poem in question is apparently "Fern Hill," Thomas's lyric evocation of youthful innocence, and this text offers an illuminating commentary on Mason's story. Although the poem celebrates the lush beauty of a boy's farm home and his total harmony with that environment, several lines warn of imminent change. In the midst of his joy, the boy is both green and dying. Such prelapsarian glory cannot last, and the boy must eventually leave his paradise. In like manner Mary's Edenic interlude in "Residents and Transients" will also be brief. Living in the midst of a garden, she enjoys only a short period of bliss before her expulsion into a world of pain and further travels.

This pain comes appropriately with a horrible image on the road itself. As Mary drives along with her lover one night, she suddenly sees an injured rabbit on the pavement: "It is hopping in place, the way runners will run in place. Its forelegs are frantically working, but its rear end has been smashed and it cannot get out of the road" (*S*, 130). This graphic image eerily combines impetus and impotence. The dying rabbit still tries desperately to travel but is powerless to do so. In its fusion of stasis and frenetic activity, the rabbit is emblematic of many Mason characters who cannot resolve conflicts, either internal or external, about travel and home. Like many transients the rabbit hops furiously but never progresses. Like some residents it is firmly attached to a specific place but still intensely motivated to go elsewhere. This vivid depiction of the struggling rabbit exemplifies what Raymond Carver has termed the "aftereffect image" in Mason's fiction.[50] Long after one reads the story, such a defining image persists like a picture burned into one's retina.

Seeing this tortured rabbit ends Mary's idyllic summer. In reluctantly promising to join her husband in Louisville, Mary has not really resolved the dilemma between residence and transience but only acknowledged its painful reality. As evidence of Mary's continuing confusion, Mason ends the story with an ambiguous travel image. Mary's cat Brenda has eyes of two different colors. On this particular occasion, because of an accident of illumination, "her blue eye shines red and her yellow eye shines green" (*S*, 131), reminding Mary of a traffic light. If Mary (like Beverly in "Memphis") is at a crucial intersection of life, this strange traffic light offers contradictory signals. If she heeds the green light, she will presumably abandon her rural home and move briskly along to her husband in Louisville. If she obeys the red light instead, she may come to a full stop and avoid the frequent transfers of Stephen's transient life. In her indecision Mary finds herself "waiting for the light to change" (131)—to provide a different or at least an unambiguous command. As Darlene Reimers Hill has stated, Mary "would like to have an absolute sign," but Mason, "in her artistic wisdom, will not give Mary—or us—that clear signal" (Darlene Hill, 89).

Cultivators of Their Own Gardens: Invoking the Pastoral

As a child Mason spent many summer days working in her family's vegetable garden. Later, as a graduate student in English, she wrote a dissertation focusing on the literary significance of gardens in Nabokov's *Ada*. Well acquainted with gardens on both a concrete and a metaphorical level, Mason uses them significantly in her own fiction. Just as early settlers in America sought refuge in a New World Eden, several protagonists in Mason's stories attempt to create their own limited versions of prelapsarian order.

Mason has noted that a garden is "a microcosm, a miniature realm in which ideally all is ordered, fruitful, and beautiful."[51] In sharp contrast, Mason's characters may inhabit a landscape characterized by disorder, abortive hopes, and ugly social change. As we have seen, many characters may flee this landscape in search of a more harmonious domain, but some resist the urge to wander and remain at home to cultivate their own gardens. The word *telos* is etymologically akin to both the Greek word for wheel (*kyklos*) and the Latin word for cultivate (*colere*). Accordingly, the strong teleological impulse in Mason's characters displays itself both in travel and in tending the vegetable patch. Like the traveler Liz in "Sorghum," Mason's gardeners obviously seek more than food. Mason observes that "idealized gardens have traditionally been the literary locations of human paradises, the premier example of which, for our own culture, is the Garden of Eden. In that paradise, everything, including man, occupies a secure and rightful position in the divine order" (*Garden*, 15). Mason's gardeners hardly expect to re-create paradise, but they do seek evidence of order within a limited territory.

Leo Marx has distinguished between two modes of the pastoral. The sentimental pastoral displays a "simple, affirmative attitude" toward traditional rural values, but the complex pastoral qualifies or ironically questions the notion of "peace and harmony in a green pasture."[52] As a Southerner who grew up on a farm, Mason is heir to a culture that long valued the rural over the urban, the agrarian over the industrial. As a trendy contemporary writer whose works chronicle the latest fads of American popular culture, she is acutely aware of the threats and alternatives to traditional lifestyles. In explaining why she and her siblings left the family farm, Mason says that they "didn't want to be slaves to nature"—that "maintaining the Garden of Eden was too much work" ("Way," 94). At the same time she expresses profound respect for the labors of her father—the "slow enduring pace of regular toil and the habit of mind that goes with it, the habit of knowing what is lasting and of noting every nuance of soil and water and season" (96).

Mason's works develop contrapuntal patterns by playing the old pastoral ideal against antipastoral skepticism about the continued feasibility of that ideal. At some points her characters may indeed reduce their problems to green thoughts within a green shade, but this pastoral solution obtains in only a few cases.

"Offerings" (1980)

"I declare, Sandy Lee, you have moved plumb out into the wilderness" (*S*, 54), announces the grandmother of the main character in "Offerings." Sandra has abandoned the city and a troubled marriage for the solitude of her rural home, but in trying to ground herself in the basics, she becomes atavistic. In her isolation Sandra moves beyond the pastoral and approaches the feral.

Just as her grandmother declares, Sandra actually lives not amidst a well-tended garden but in a wild place. Throughout American literature, from Rip Van Winkle to Updike's Rabbit Angstrom, a male protagonist is typically the character in flight from commitment to marriage—a culture's most elemental unit of social responsibility. Such is certainly the case in several Mason stories, like "Still Life with Watermelon" and "Hunktown." There, steady female characters tend to hearth and home while their confused mates wander. In this story, however, the female character seeks home by lighting out for the territories. In her hurt and anger Sandra holes up in the woods, and the physical wilderness all around her corresponds to the emotional wilderness within. Mason has commented that the story began with disconnected images like the body of a dead bird on a stump and clumps of ragweed. As the plot developed, it became a study of Sandra being "torn between the demands of the natural world, which seemed overgrown ... and the demands of the social world."[53]

In Sandra's house, yard, and garden everything steadily reverts to its primitive state, and she takes "a perverse delight" (*S*, 54) in the regression. Despite her grandmother's warning that dust bunnies will multiply and soon take over, Sandra never dusts. Spiders reclaim territory, and their webs dangle from ceilings. Outside the house the boundary between civilized and savage is also blurred. Sandra has not mowed the grass in weeks, and clumps of ragweed punctuate what was once lawn. Even the beauty of flowering plants around the house is largely accidental. When Sandra's mother praises her pretty cosmos, Sandra replies, "They're volunteers. I didn't do a thing" (58). In this revealing exchange, the botanical name "cosmos" suggests a pun. The blossoms in Sandra's garden are serendipitous, just as the order in her universe is very uncertain.

In the foreground of Sandra's world, untended nature is ragged but safe. In the distance, however, it is red in tooth and claw. Sandra must repeatedly count her cats to make sure another has not been killed in the woods. Meanwhile, the cats themselves slaughter birds, moles, and other creatures. Sandra guards her ducks from attack by foxes, and at night she frequently hears "their menacing yaps echoing on the hillside" (*S*, 59). Recently she has also heard the cry of a wildcat like "a baby screaming in terror" (59). Instead of scaring Sandra, this sound thrills her, and she listens for it again every night. She appreciates the high drama of the wild but does not fully understand its ferocity. She takes pride in living independently in the woods but is ill prepared for the rigors of nature. The time of the story is late summer, but Sandra's woodpile is low, and she has not taken time to insulate her attic or fix a leak in her basement.

In preferring her garden to the big-city bars frequented by her husband, Jerry, Sandra's values (like those of Joann in "Hunktown") are solid and unimpeachable, but in virtually abandoning all society and courting the savage, her actions are extreme. Her only social contacts during the story are with her mother and grandmother, who come for a brief visit. Even during this visit Sandra's perspective is atavistic. She stays in the kitchen cooking tomato sauce that reminds her of "bowls of blood" (*S*, 58) while Mama and Grandmother watch the movie *That's Entertainment!* on television. With scenes of Fred Astaire dancing with Eleanor Powell and of Esther Williams and her troupe performing an elaborate water ballet, this movie offers a sharp contrast to Sandra's present situation. While she lives in stark isolation, the graceful dancing is an elaborate ritual of social interaction. While she submits to the randomness of wild nature, the water ballet exhibits artifice and careful control. From the kitchen Sandra occasionally peeks at scenes of the movie, but she remains strangely removed from this realm. The movie on television displays spectacular illusions; Sandra's recent actions suggest delusion. The movie illusions are clearly recognizable as art, but Sandra fails to recognize her delusions and realize their potential dangers.

Sandra may readily delude herself because she has long been a party to deception. For years she and her mother have hidden harsh truths from Grandmother Stamper. As an odd prelude to Sandra's story, "Offerings" provides a graphic account of her mother's hysterectomy. The story describes the surgery in bloody detail, but Mama has never let Grandmother Stamper know that she even had an operation. For 25 years she has also concealed her smoking from Grandmother, and now she and Sandra hide the truth about Sandra's separation.

Because of such deceptions, Grandmother Stamper never confronts certain painful realities, and Sandra also fails to see her own situation clearly. She begs Grandmother Stamper "to talk about the past, to tell about the farm Sandra can barely remember" (*S*, 56). Since the farm is so remote in time, Sandra romanticizes it and loves to hear stories glorifying rural life. In like manner her romantic visions of nature's delicate beauty obscure the potential savagery in her current environment. Juxtaposed with the terrible scream of the wildcat is Sandra's lyrical description of spiderwebs in the field: "In the early morning the dew shines on their trampolines, and she can imagine bouncing with an excited spring from web to web, all the way up the hill to the woods" (59). Tina Bucher interprets this passage as a metaphor for connections among women (especially mother and daughter) that illustrates their power to sustain each other in times of crisis. In asserting that the story ends "beautifully" and "positively," Bucher overlooks the ominous overtones of this elaborate fairy-tale image.[54] In the spiderweb conceit, Sandra sees herself moving not toward social involvement but deeper into the lonely woods. Furthermore, her means of getting there is frail and insubstantial. Instead of bouncing her to ever greater heights, the flimsy webs would surely break and cling. Sandra's trampoline metaphor in this "fantasy of escape" is remarkably inventive, but it fails to displace the more conventional image of the spiderweb as trap.[55] Although she may not realize it, Sandra is more caught in a web than soaring above it.

The title of this story identifies one further evidence of Sandra's disorientation. After struggling to protect her ducks from foxes, Sandra decides that she "would not mind" (*S*, 59) if a wildcat devoured them.

For this creature the ducks would be "her offering" (59). Sandra has long been a cat lover, but such reverence for the wild rather than the domestic variety seems extreme. In deliberately giving up her ducks to the predator, she would not just be living in harmony with nature. Instead she would be surrendering to its wildness. Such an action suggests a futile attempt to appease the mysterious forces beyond human understanding or control.

In the later story "Bumblebees," Mason shows how a retreat to a farm and pastoral activities can produce emotional healing. In her own rural setting Sandra may eventually discover such means for rejuvenation. At the moment, however, her anger is too intense and her confusion too great. Instead of cultivating her garden, she is merely wandering in the wilderness.

"Hunktown" (1984)

The action in "Hunktown" moves from a turnip patch in Kentucky to the Bluebird Lounge in Nashville. It juxtaposes old-fashioned pastoral values with honky-tonk glitz. Beneath an expanse of flashy surfaces, Joann Swann tries to locate some solid core. In the midst of much that is fleeting, she seeks a foundation that will endure.

The hunk of the story is Cody Swann, Joann's middle-aged husband, who still proclaims that "good-lookin" is his middle name (*LL*, 38). Laid off after almost 20 years at a local factory, Cody drinks and plans his second career as a country-music star. When he gets a temporary gig at a club in Nashville, he urges Joann to give up her job at the post office, sell the family farm she has inherited, and move with him to Music City.

This family dilemma establishes a crucial debate about the true meaning of "country." For Cody the essence of country is found in songs "about fickle women and trucks and heartache" (*LL*, 35). Its mecca is Nashville, its shrine is the Ryman Auditorium, and its high priests are such performers as Webb Pierce, Ernest Tubb, and Hank Williams. Joann fears that this popular sense of the word has displaced a more important meaning. She subscribes to a definition of "country" that emphasizes rural roots, concern for the land, and respect for the bounty that land produces.

Joann is a thoroughly modern woman, but several scenes display her continuing closeness to the land. Early in the story she goes with her daughter, Patty, to a truck patch to pick turnip greens. Highly knowledgeable about vegetables and food preservation, Joann offers her daughter detailed instructions about picking greens. Although some of the turnips are "large enough to pull" (*LL,* 36), the trick is to strip off the leaves without getting down into the stalk. This way one can harvest the tops without disturbing the edible roots. Patty, in her high heels, is absurdly out of place in this vegetable patch. She can't tell a turnip green from a weed and complains that the fuzzy leaves sting her hands.

Patty's ineptness and indifference to the country lore of an earlier generation indicate her own lack of sustaining roots. Unlike her mother, who carefully leaves the turnip roots intact, Patty is sadly detached from her past. She is country not in the pastoral but in the flighty honky-tonk sense of the term. In fact, the story of her short life could provide the texts for several country-music songs. Her misfortunes to date include teen pregnancy, shotgun marriage, spontaneous abortion after being hit by a falling hay bale, divorce after the birth of two children, and three automobile accidents. Patty may yet inspire a sad country song because she habitually flirts with her songwriting stepfather, Cody, and he affirms that Trouble is her middle name.

When Joann laments that people "can't hold together anymore" (*LL,* 45), Patty becomes a prime example. Having divorced her husband, Patty maintains a tenuous connection with the two small children that her marriage produced. She casually leaves them behind with Joann when a new boyfriend invites her to go to St. Louis. Without roots to connect her to the past, she cannot learn from it. Even after three accidents, she still refuses to fasten her seat belt. To hide scars on her forehead, the lingering evidence of one recent accident, she simply combs her hair a new way.

Even though Joann worries about an adult child without roots, her childish husband is a greater concern. According to Debbie, a cocktail waitress at the Bluebird Lounge, "men are such little boys" (*LL,* 42), and among the numerous boy-men in Mason's stories, Cody Swann is one of the most immature as well as most charming. He lives with Joann on the old homeplace, but for him it is a location to inhabit briefly and leave behind. Joann acknowledges that Cody is no farmer, but she still grieves because the "field where her father used to grow turnips" is now "spotted with burdock and thistles" while Cody is "away in Nashville, seeking fame" (37). Cody is so enthralled with his musical career that he neglects all other responsibilities. He tills the garden but does it so hurriedly that it looks "as though cows had trampled the ground" (37). He hangs a new door but pieces together the facing and leaves a big crack where cold air enters. Even his voice reminds Joann of an unfinished task. It bubbles along not like a pristine spring but like the tank of a toilet that runs until its handle is jiggled.

Cody's voice is like water that runs incessantly but not very deep, and many details of his musical career display superficiality—the shallowness of his roots. For his gig at the Bluebird Lounge, he buys a flashy new suit with fringed pants and a vest decorated with butterflies. In this new outfit he preens and postures like the elegant bird whose name he shares. Ironically, though, this fancy costume hardly contains a not so attractive reality. Cody's pants are too small, and his beer gut almost breaks through. Just as the costume is more surface than substance, Cody is preoccupied with the cover of the new album he paid to record. If the record doesn't sell, he will proudly frame the cover and hang it in his den. Even his technique of recording suggests shallow self-absorption. When Joann hears a backup vocal in which Cody sings along with himself, she finds it "self-indulgent and private, like masturbation" (*LL,* 39).

If the errant male is a recurring figure in American literature from Rip Van Winkle onward, this stereotype is even more pervasive in country music lyrics from Hank Williams to the Outlaws. Note, for example, titles like "A Good-Hearted Woman in Love with a Good-Timing Man," sung by Waylon Jennings and Willie Nelson. Such lyrics become apt texts for Cody's new career as he begins to live his art. In a curious twist, Bobbie Ann Mason's name has surfaced as the title of a recent song chronicling the waywardness of still another man. In the song "Bobbie Ann Mason," performed by Rick Trevino, an adult male reflects on his poor grades in high school. He excuses his failure to get any education simply because he sat right behind Miss Bobbie Ann Mason—a scholarly but sexy teen who was both too cute and too cool. Of this accidentally eponymous lyric Mason has commented: "I'm not sure why he's singing about me, but I won't argue. Ditty immortality is mine."[56] Actually the songwriter had in mind an old girlfriend whose name didn't fit his melody. Since he liked the sound of "Bobbie Ann Mason," he simply plugged in that name.

As the loyal wife so often celebrated in country music, Joann usually goes with Cody as he flits off to Nashville for brief performances, but she remains firmly rooted in the soil of her homeplace. The oxymoronic name of the Bluebird Lounge never deceives her. Although the ornithological reference may suggest sylvan felicity, Joann clearly sees the place as just a bar with fake country decor. After one weekend at the Bluebird, she returns to her garden "with a sense of urgency" (*LL,* 42). She gathers the last vegetables, collects pole beans "to save for seed" (42), and pulls up dying plants. During these autumn days Joann feels a deep need to gather food and prepare appropriately for the coming winter. In saving seed she even anticipates a new cycle of life with next year's planting. While Cody expends and dissipates, she carefully puts away. Cody (basking in the endless summer of the Bluebird Lounge) resembles the foolish grasshopper in Aesop's fable, and Joann is like the industrious ant. In this case the fact that the two are married to each other creates added dissonance.

By embracing the basics of life, Joann offers a powerful critique of the clichés so prevalent in Cody's songs. When Cody sings the defiant country classic "I'd Rather Die Young," Joann hears a story of "pointless suffering" (*LL*, 39). Instead of capturing life's essential struggles, such lyrics reflect only maudlin self-indulgence. In her own situation Joann could follow the simplistic advice of another well-known song and stand by her man. Debbie, however, warns against being "caught in one cliché or another" (47). Having heard hundreds of country songs while working at the Bluebird, she knows their inconsistencies: "They tell you to stand by your man, but then they say he's just going to use you somehow" (46). Such pseudowisdom is no substitute for the more profound truths of Joann's garden and homeplace.

Cody's youthful good looks have long nourished his hopes, but the story ends with a definite emphasis on mortality. After years of smoking, Cody's father develops lung cancer, and Cody must leave the Bluebird to visit him in a Memphis hospital. All along Joann has been disposing of dead plants and calmly preparing for winter, but this sudden proximity to death shocks Cody. At the same time the photograph for his album cover is a terrible disappointment. Although Cody stands under a neon sign that reads "Hunktown" and wears a Hunktown T-shirt, he no longer looks young and handsome.

Such harsh lessons may force Cody to look deeper. Just as this story develops a more profound definition of "country," it may also suggest multiple meanings of the term "hunk." The base meaning of the term is simply a large lump. Stripped of the surface glamour that Cody values so highly, a hunk is nothing more than a formless mass. Giving that mass a significant shape is Cody's immediate task as he grows inevitably older.

"Bumblebees" (1987)

In evoking the beauties of nature, "Bumblebees" is Mason's most lyrical story. It describes in exquisite detail a freckled sparrow egg, the lacy pink blossoms of an apricot tree, and a thistle flower as soft as duck down. The story even quotes Wordsworth's "Michael"—a poem in the pastoral tradition where nature provides consolation in times of loss. In this catalog of nature's beauties, however, Mason does not ignore its destructive force. Characters in this story must learn to appreciate what is lovely and benign but also to accommodate much that is loathsome and brutal.

The two main characters are middle-aged women who for the past two years have been living together on a small farm and "rebuilding their lives" (*LL*, 101). Barbara is recovering from a bitter divorce and Ruth from the shock of an automobile accident that killed her husband and daughter. A third, less troubled character living on the farm temporarily is Barbara's daughter, Allison. Allison has just broken up with her boyfriend and is considering dropping out of college. Even the dog adopted by these women has obvious wounds. It is a skinny stray with a laceration on a foreleg that it has licked raw. This open sore, which Allison bandages with a sanitary napkin, parallels the lingering problems of the three women, especially Ruth's chronic grief.

Three years after the accident, Ruth's grief remains pathological. In one persistent ritual of mourning, she studies pictures of her husband and daughter, shuffles them, and spreads them out on her bed "like cards in a game of solitaire" (*LL*, 112). In this case the idiosyncratic card game does little to amuse Ruth or relieve her desperate sense of isolation. To fill the void left after her daughter's death, Ruth appropriates Allison as an object of affection and abnormal concern. She can't sleep until Allison comes home at night, she pokes through Allison's personal property, and she even pilfers small items. Like the parasites around the farm, she feeds on others to sustain herself. Ironically, when Ruth sprays a peach tree to kill borers, she stands downwind and the insecticide covers her. In her self-accusatory grief she continues to poison herself.

As therapy for their various hurts, the women repair the old farmhouse and, like Candide, cultivate their garden. In its original condition the decrepit house is an obvious correlative of Barbara and Ruth's damaged psyches. Cracks mar floors and walls; broken appliances and unidentifiable parts litter the attic. In one closet dried husks of dead bumblebees serve as reminders of mortality and as ominous warnings that, in the aftermath of trauma, Barbara and Ruth could themselves become empty shells. Eventually the women clear away litter, caulk cracks, hang storm windows, and install new plasterboard. With these repairs the old house is still flawed but certainly more solid and secure.

Outside Barbara and Ruth plant a garden and an orchard and perse-
vere long enough to enjoy their fruits. For Barbara in particular, moving
to the farm is a return to the sources of her life. She grew up in the
country and has lived too long "in a space too small for a garden" (*LL*,
101). She is eager to plant again and, as evidence of her steady focus on
the future rather than the past, she envisions beds of hardy perennials.
As in *Spence + Lila* a well-tended garden becomes a refuge from pain
and a possible antidote against future hurt. In their vegetable garden
Barbara teaches Allison how to sucker tomatoes. If she pinches away
new leaves where the branches fork, the plants will produce more fruit.
Barbara cannot explain this mystery of reduction to achieve increase,
but she fully appreciates its paradoxical truth.

If Barbara cannot comprehend nature's mysterious bounty, neither
can she understand its grim destructiveness. Moles tunnel among the
roots of their vegetables while bugs and caterpillars eat away at the
leaves. Early in the story drought bakes the earth and plants wither.
When the rain finally comes, it allows weeds to flourish in the mud and
mold to creep through the house. Barbara digs trenches in an attempt to
divert floodwater from the plants, but eventually water covers the garden and she simply decides to plant on higher ground next year. In her
efforts to nourish both her plants and her human companions, Barbara
feels that she is "tending too many gardens" and everything is "growing
in some sick or stunted way" (*LL*, 112).

One result of the continued rain is a fantastic display of mushrooms.
For Barbara this unexpected burst of beauty is "a magical but clumsy
compensation for the ruined garden" (*LL*, 113). Through this profusion
of exotic shapes and brilliant colors, nature displays its creative power
even in the midst of destruction. Planted among all this beauty, however, is one small warning of nature's ambivalence. As Barbara revels in
the glorious spectacle, she carefully sidesteps a bunch of ugly black
mushrooms that look dangerous.

If the various mushrooms hint at nature's ambivalence, bumblebees
provide much stronger evidence. References to bees hover throughout
the story and invite divergent readings. Bees trapped behind the house's
new siding are analogous to Barbara and Ruth trapped in their emotional
distress. Bees waking up after the long winter and creeping sluggishly
about suggest the women's gradual recuperation. The bee's sting is an
obvious example of sharp pain inflicted without warning. Having suf-
fered the metaphorical sting of death, Ruth is especially fearful of a possible bee sting and won't even wear her glasses outdoors because the

tiny R in the corner of the lens reminds her of a bee. When a bee does sting Allison, Ruth can hardly tolerate the pain of merely observing. Barbara soothes her daughter and assures her that the pain "won't last" (*LL*, 108), just as she tries to convince Ruth that the sting of death will not endure forever.

Although bees can cause temporary discomfort, they serve an important function in nature's scheme. They pollinate flowers and fruit trees to insure that they will be productive. The same bees that Ruth fears so intensely "zoom through the garden, like truck drivers on an interstate, on their way to . . . exotic blossoms" (*LL*, 103). When the rains end, "the bumblebees, solar-activated, buzz through the orchard" (113). Despite her fears Ruth is beginning to accept incongruities like that embodied in the bumblebee. After three years she can almost laugh about one detail of the accident that killed her husband and daughter. The truck that hit them broadside was full of turnips. Death amid apples or watermelons might have been tragic, but the mortal blow inflicted by a load of turnips seems merely ludicrous. In either case, however, pastoral bounty subsumes the horror of death. Ruth is now able to appreciate God's beauties and, to an extent, his strange jokes.

As Annette Kolodny has pointed out, traditional versions of the pastoral in America have been male-centered and patriarchal. The myth of America as the New World Eden assumed that the land was virginal and that man's purpose (indeed, his manifest destiny) was to possess it. If a woman was not mere property to assist in this appropriation of the land, then she became (especially in Southern literature) little more than a decorative flower in the garden.[57]

Elizabeth Jane Harrison argues that Southern women writers from Ellen Glasgow to Alice Walker have challenged this male version of the pastoral and attempted to establish an alternative. Such a liberated view of the pastoral may experiment with gender roles and "explore female autonomy in rural settings." Harrison alludes briefly to Mason but claims that her stories fail to depict "a woman protagonist as empowered by her relationship to the land."[58] In a landscape rapidly being paved over with highways and shopping center parking lots, most of Mason's women are indeed unable to connect with the land around them. It is notable, however, that only the women make any significant attempt to do so. Mary in "Residents and Transients" and Sandra in "Offerings" aspire to pastoral autonomy (while their men dash off to the big city), but their successes are limited. Joann in "Hunktown" is a successful gardener who draws both physical and spiritual sustenance from the soil, but she remains largely isolated in her pursuits. Her husband and daughter gravitate toward urban excitement, and her only real confidante is a Nashville cocktail waitress. In "Bumblebees" three women live and work together to reclaim a run-down farm, and in doing so they realize a sense of community. Lucinda Hardwick MacKethan says that the pastoral ideal in Southern literature—the dream of Arcady—always implied a cohesive social order as well as a close relationship of an individual with the land.[59] Among Mason's gardeners only the women in "Bumblebees" come close to achieving this ideal.

In their struggles these three women challenge the old stereotype of a community of females as "an austere banishment from both social power and biological rewards."[60] Nina Auerbach shows that such a negative stereotype goes back as far as the myths of the Graie (three maimed sisters who shared a single eye) and the Gorgons (another triad of hideous sisters). Mason's triad of women is also isolated from the larger society, and each is scarred from past hurts. Nevertheless, their pastoral activities help to define a new community and anchor it securely in the nourishing soil.

Craftspeople and Artists: Assembling the Parts of a Coherent Whole

Confronting problems and confusion in their immediate surroundings, Mason's travelers try to discover order by going elsewhere. Mason's gardeners perceive similar problems but attempt to find harmony in the beauty, bounty, and timeless patterns of nature. Several stories display a third response to this basic dilemma. In this third group of stories, craftspeople and aspiring artists take the jumbled parts of life and try to create a coherent whole—a garden of the mind.

Of course, Mason herself toiled as a gardener and explored as a traveler before becoming an accomplished artist. In her study of Nabokov, she suggests a close connection between artists and gardeners. "A work of art," she says, "is like an imaginary garden." An artist "creates a work of art as a gardener plans and prunes a beautiful garden." The finished artwork is "a miniature version of Eden, the best product of the imagination" (*Garden*, 121). Mason even asserts that the successful artist achieves a kind of divinity—the only return to Eden that is available to man (155).

Just as Mason's praise of the artist is high, her definition is broad. Among those who re-create versions of Eden, she would include not just writers and painters but also scientists and mathematicians. Rather than actually discovering laws of nature, such thinkers merely posit new patterns—new holds for grappling with the ultimate "mysteries of . . . spirit" (*Garden*, 69). Scientists, like all other artists, impose order on the world by the force of their imagination, and the "putative Newtonian/Einsteinian universe" is merely one vision of order that will ultimately be supplanted by a more comprehensive vision (69).

Aware that any true appreciation of a work of art is itself an act of creation, Mason even classifies the appreciator (reader, viewer, listener, etc.) as an artist. To the extent that we comprehend a work of art and perceive its patterns, we share in the creative process and "can taste some of the bliss" of the return to Eden (*Garden*, 155).

In her analysis of Mason's novel *In Country*, Barbara Ryan argues that Samantha Hughes progresses from a structuralist to a poststructuralist stage in her reading of the world around her. At first Sam assumes the existence of an unchanging, suprahuman authority whose discovery would automatically provide order and meaning. In her search for a father, she also seeks this more comprehensive Logos. Eventually Sam realizes that "no Logos is available" to offer "a ready-made pattern of coherence and significance." Instead, she must accept "her personal role in the co-production of meaning, coherence, a self."[61]

Several of Mason's stories imply a similar progression from structuralist to poststructuralist assumptions. In many cases Mason's travelers are quasi structuralists who seek order and authority external to themselves. From the immature Steve in "Midnight Magic" to the elderly Crittendons in "The Ocean," such travelers ply the highways but never attain an ordered destination. Mason's craftspeople and aspiring artists know little about metaphysics and critical theory, but their tacit principles of operation are poststructuralist. Their artistic achievements may be humble, but in the creative endeavor itself they are active participants in the process of forging meaning.

Despite the provincial context of Mason's stories, would-be artists and art appreciators are numerous. Mason says that in graduate school she had her fill of one character type common in elitist fiction. Thoroughly tired of the sensitive young man, the alienated artist with a superior sensibility, she chose to write instead about store clerks and truck drivers whose lives are equally valid and complicated. Mason further asserts that such characters can be as sensitive as the stereotyped artist hero (Havens, 95–96). At the most mundane level Mason's down-home artists are craftspeople like Leroy in "Shiloh" who buy and assemble craft kits to produce plastic models, needlepoint pillows, or string art. Even if these kits are mass-produced, their assembly requires a creative effort—some attempt to put together the pieces of life's puzzle. Other assemblers, slightly more original than Leroy in their artistic media and their final products, include the woodworker Mack in "The Rookers" and the seamstress Cleo in "Old Things." Amid such craftspeople we also find an aspiring painter; Louise in "Still Life with Watermelon" works with colors and shapes, light and shadow, but her basic task is still composition—how to arrange parts to create a coherent whole. For some of Mason's artists, most notably Donald in "Big Bertha Stories" and Lynnette in "Coyotes," the chosen medium is words. Unable to discover the ultimate Logos, these compulsive storytellers assemble lesser words to spin fantastic narratives. The most prominent art appreciators in Mason's stories focus on still another art form—popular music. Edwin in "A New-Wave Format" eventually perceives order in apparently chaotic new-wave songs, and Opal in "Love Life" discovers wisdom in the puzzling images of music videos.

"Shiloh" (1980)

"Shiloh" is Mason's most frequently anthologized story, and as such it provides a good introduction to her work. Like many of her other stories, it is set in a small Kentucky town and contains pervasive allusions to popular culture. The central characters are young adults experiencing marital problems and other disturbing effects of rapid social change.

The Moffitts have not, like Mason, traveled from Kentucky to New York City, but culture shock has come home to them. Change has invaded and transformed their small town. Once farmers sat around the courthouse square playing checkers and spitting tobacco juice. Now subdivisions spread like oil slicks across the countryside, and the teenaged son of a local physician sells pot in the shopping center parking lot. Once gender roles were clearly defined, with the man as king of his castle. Now Norma Jean looks like Wonder Woman as she pumps iron while Leroy—in ironic contrast to his regal name—sits meekly on the sofa and does needlepoint. In the old days marriages and truths were lasting. Today divorce is commonplace, and the community's collective wisdom is only as old as the last Donahue show.

For Leroy change comes dramatically with a highway accident that ends his stint as a long-distance truck driver. Now his wrecked tractor-trailer rig sits as a foreboding symbol in the backyard, and Leroy tries to sort through the wreckage of his personal life. Physical therapy helps to strengthen Leroy's body, but no effective therapy is available for his damaged psyche. A small metal pin holds Leroy's hip together, but his link with his wife becomes increasingly strained and artificial.

Perhaps Leroy wrecks his truck because for 15 years he has been speeding headlong down the wrong road. Although Leroy's truck has taken him far away from Kentucky, he has never escaped the memory of a dead baby or the resulting problems in his marriage. When the wreck ends his days as a traveler and brings him home permanently, Leroy feels that he and Norma Jean "are waking up out of a dream together" (*S*, 3). They are together again as in the early days of their marriage, and he uneasily "wonders if one of them should mention the child" (2–3).

Instead of talking about this problem, however, Leroy and Norma Jean follow parallel but separate paths. With his truck torn apart and his life fragmented, Leroy tries to create order in miniature. Mason's working title for this story was "Constructions," and she originally saw it as an account of "people who constructed their realities" (Dorothy Hill, 99). Leroy's artistic constructions include a tiny log cabin made from prenotched Popsicle sticks, a B-17 Flying Fortress from snap-together parts, a string-art sailing ship, and a lamp with a model truck as its base. All these creations apparently begin as craft kits—prepackaged collections of parts with printed direction sheets indicating exactly how they should fit together. By transforming isolated components into a finished whole, Leroy performs a ritualistic act, and what he accomplishes on a small scale he hopes to project magically into life size. These mundane craft projects are the contemporary equivalents of what Arnold van Gennep has termed sympathetic rites—ceremonies "based on belief in the reciprocal action of like on like, of opposite on opposite, of the container and the contained . . . of image and real object or real being."[62] Barbara Henning argues that the building images gain power because they are more than "textual figures, supplied by the author." Instead, the various construction activities "are presented metonymically as multiple stories, anecdotes, examples, and details coming from the domain or context of the narrative."[63]

Leroy's tiny Popsicle-stick cabin reminds him of a nativity scene, and he decides to build a full-scale log cabin as a home where his marriage can be reborn. As in his craft kits the components of this log home will come precut and numbered, eliminating any possible messiness and uncertainty. Leroy thinks that he and Norma Jean can raise the cabin together and thus revert to a simpler time when solid pioneer values prevailed. In preparation for the cabin raising, Leroy studies blueprints and even practices with Lincoln Logs, but he is afraid to move from ritual to reality—from his toys to the problems of full-scale construction.

Norma Jean has no sympathy for Leroy's scheme to build a cabin but actively pursues her own ritualistic patterns. In building a new body, she hopes to create a new identity. With her double given name Norma Jean may sound like a good old girl, but she is clearly striving to become a new woman. In addition to working out, Norma Jean also makes music. As a contrast to the discordant notes all around her, she creates pleasing harmonies on a new electric organ. With its "optional flute, violin, trumpet, clarinet, and banjo" (*S*, 3) the single instrument becomes an entire orchestra and gives the illusion of many components merging together even when Norma Jean plays in solitude. Furthermore, the "preset chords" (3) on the organ provide the same security as the directions for assembly in Leroy's craft kits. The most obvious example of Norma Jean's ritualistic efforts to create order is her work in an adult-education course. The class is composition, and in it she learns to construct outlines that are paradigms of careful organization. Unfortunately, the clarity of her outlines far exceeds that of her life.

Through their ritualistic acts of assembling log cabins and outlines, Leroy and Norma Jean create a semblance of order, but such actions are only temporary measures. Their critical task is to put together fragments of time into a coherent personal history. They can hold together as a couple only if they can bridge the painful gaps and unite the disconnected stages of their individual lives. In only 16 years Leroy moves from carefree teenager to young father, from grieving parent to absentee husband, from macho trucker to disabled house spouse. Since unexpected occurrences (namely, a pregnancy, a death, and a traffic accident) make each of these shifts so sudden, the transitions are especially jagged and painful. Pulled in so many directions, Leroy cannot integrate the separate parts of his life into a coherent whole. Like an undertow, his own accident pulls him back to the time of Randy's death, but the fragments of time don't fit neatly together.

Norma Jean's personal history is equally incoherent. Although she creates harmonious music on the electric organ, she cannot harmonize her separate roles as daughter, young mother, and wife. As an adult Norma Jean has been smoking for years, but she cowers like a disobedient child when her mother, Mabel, catches her in the act. Instead of progressing steadily through time, Norma Jean is caught in a regressive loop and feels like a teenager once again. Mabel's displeasure with her daughter's smoking is actually a token of much deeper resentment. Mabel continues to blame Norma Jean for her premarital sex and pregnancy, and as punishment for such adult activity she refuses to let Norma Jean grow up. By telling a story about a dog killing a baby and suggesting that Norma Jean was also a neglectful mother, Mabel reduces her to an incompetent child. Adrienne Rich observes that nothing in human nature is "more resonant with charges than the flow of energy between two biologically alike bodies, one of whom has lain in amniotic bliss inside the other, one of which has labored to give birth to the other."[64] For Norma Jean this cathexis becomes grim conflict—"a struggle with a bond that is powerful and painful, that threatens engulfment and self-loss."[65]

In their failure to compose either a personal or a collective history, Leroy and Norma Jean display a problem common in Mason's stories and in postmodern society. Fredric Jameson identifies as two major features of postmodernism "the transformation of reality into images" and "the fragmentation of time into a series of perpetual presents."[66] In a similar vein Robert Brinkmeyer describes Mason's fictional realm as a "society cut off from traditions whose denizens live in a continuous present and grapple less with problems of right and wrong than with matters of technological progress and utility."[67] Such a generalization goes too far, but Brinkmeyer is right in noting that Mason's characters seek guidance not from their elders but from contemporary pop culture oracles like Phil Donahue and Erma Bombeck. In this world cut off from its roots, "trends instead of traditions hold sway" (Brinkmeyer, 1987, 22).

Norma Jean finally breaks out of her time loop on a trip into the past. Failing to achieve order and harmony in their varied artistic endeavors, Norma Jean and Leroy become travelers. They head to Shiloh for a second honeymoon, even though this site of an especially bloody battle seems an unlikely place to find marital peace. At Shiloh, Norma Jean walks confidently through a cemetery, finally indicating her readiness to move beyond Randy's death. As the story ends, she stands on a bluff "looking out over the Tennessee River" (*S*, 16). Mason has commented that many readers mistakenly see this detail as a suggestion of suicide. She vehemently objects to such a reading and asserts that Norma Jean's "life is on the way up" (Wilhelm, 1988, 35). The key detail in the text is that Norma Jean is looking out over the river, not down into it. The river is a sharp dividing line between past and future, and with her vision clearly focused on the opposite bank Norma Jean is ready to transcend the currents of time. Her famous namesake, Norma Jean Baker, could not in the end cope with her identity as Marilyn Monroe and did commit suicide. Norma Jean Moffitt is determined to cross her river and explore all the possibilities on the other side.

If Norma Jean is about to escape her time loop, Leroy's fate is uncertain. He has spent many years on the road in his truck, but on the way to Shiloh he is a passive traveler. Norma Jean pilots the car, and he feels like a boring hitchhiker. In the cemetery, after saying she wants to leave him, she walks briskly away while he merely hobbles along with one leg asleep and the other injured. Norma Jean now has a clear focus on the future, but Leroy still can't get a coherent sense of history. Dazed from smoking pot, his mind blurs a Confederate raid at Shiloh with a recent drug raid back home. When he looks at Norma Jean in the distance, he can't figure out whether she is "beckoning to him" or "doing an exercise for her chest muscles" (*S*, 16). If he opts for the former interpretation, he may still awaken his leg and his mind and move alongside her toward the future. If he adopts the latter possibility, his story will loop again to the first paragraph, when Norma Jean was pumping iron and looked as formidable as Wonder Woman.

Most of Mason's stories are open-ended, and this one concludes with a highly ambiguous detail. As Norma Jean stands looking across the river and Leroy still struggles to catch up, "the sky is unusually pale—the color of the dust ruffle Mable made for their bed" (*S*, 16). Since this color was off-white, the sky is at present neither an ominous black nor an overly optimistic blue. In the future it could develop more threatening clouds, or it could clear. In comparing the color of the sky to that of a dust ruffle, Mason ends the story with an appropriate focus on the Moffitt marriage bed. In the past Mabel's dust ruffle has allowed Leroy and Norma Jean to hide unsightly things under the bed. If their marriage is to survive, they must bring hidden feelings to the surface and use the marriage bed as a place to confront their common problems.

"The Rookers" (1982)

The title story in *Shiloh* plots the fault lines in a marriage that remains intact but childless for 15 years after the death of an infant son. The next story in the collection, "The Rookers," examines strains in a somewhat older marriage that has produced three children now grown and independent. In both cases the loss of children leaves a disturbing void that threatens the marriages. The couples in the two stories are not so far apart in age. The Moffitts in "Shiloh" are 34, and the Skaggses in "The Rookers" are in their late forties. Nevertheless, the two stories are quite different in emphasis. "Shiloh" shows a couple finally completing the process of growing up while "The Rookers" displays a couple just beginning to grow old. In this respect the latter story shows kinship to a genre of fiction that Constance Rooke has labeled the *Vollendungsroman*.[68] Such stories, focusing on the completion of a life cycle rather than starting out in life, are a contemporary counterpart of the classic bildungsroman. In many such narratives the protagonist deals with concerns about the loss of youth and discovers those compensatory gifts that have been reserved for age.[69] In "The Rookers," however, Mack Skaggs makes little progress toward that discovery.

Part 1

In this story Mason gives a slightly different twist to the familiar empty nest syndrome. Here Mack, rather than his wife, Mary Lou, is the parent who suffers acutely because their three daughters have left home. Mack has great difficulty letting go of his youngest daughter because her departure to college signals for him a more general fragmentation. With Judy gone, Mack must redefine his relationship with Mary Lou and confront his own aging. As a professional cabinetmaker, Mack is skilled in joinery, the art of assembling wooden parts, but he is much less successful in pulling together the disparate elements of his life. In fact, his strategies for dealing with the disturbing changes around him are erratic and largely ineffectual. Because of a physical injury, Leroy in "Shiloh" can no longer take to the road to evade his problems. Mack is unable to assume the role of traveler because of a psychological condition. Suffering from agoraphobia, he retreats to his basement workshop as if this bunker can withstand the onslaught of change. Here he undertakes several craft projects that recall Leroy's ritualistic constructions in "Shiloh."

To supply the physical needs of his family, Mack constructs run-of-the-mill cabinets and countertops. To address his own more troubling psychological needs, he pursues various experimental woodworking projects. One such project—converting an old church pew into a dinette booth—shows the secularization of Mack's search for order. (In fact, only one story by Mason, "The Retreat," deals with organized religion, and there the church provides little real guidance. As this story's title suggests, the church offers not engagement but only the temporary safety of withdrawal.) As a sign that the old faith is inadequate for Mack, he sands the pew for hours, removing layers of finish that he equates with hypocrisy. Ironically, Mack's refinishing and recycling (to achieve the desired decorator look) suggest that the old faith is less revitalized than trivialized.

In an even more ambitious craft project, Mack symbolically confronts the forces of destruction and attempts to subvert them. Mack takes a sprocket from a bulldozer—a machine that frequently sweeps away the old to make way for new construction—and uses it as the base for a unique card table. The playing surface of this table, intended as a 25th-anniversary present for Mary Lou, is "a mosaic of wood scraps" (*S*, 18) fitted carefully together like the pieces of a crazy quilt. Having forced these odd fragments into a coherent order, Mack tries to preserve it by applying layer after layer of polyurethane. Like most artists Mack asserts that the components of the table are in themselves worthless.

Its value as a finished art object derives from "just imagination" (18). Despite all this artistic value, however, the tabletop testifies to Mack's personal failures. With only 21 pieces, it suggests "that Mack was trying to put together the years of their marriage into a convincing whole and this was as far as he got" (18). With the aura of permanence created by polyurethane, Mack's solution to life's jigsaw puzzle is like an insect encased in clear amber. Instead of a dynamic balance that leads him on through life, his order is static and arrested at too premature a stage.

Mack's craft is his primary means of seeking wholeness, but outside the workshop he pursues several other strategies to establish order and allay his fears. Even in these other pursuits his tactics are analogous to those in his woodcraft, and his failures are comparable. Mircea Eliade has noted that "the cosmogonic myth serves as the paradigm . . . for every kind of making. Nothing better ensures the success of any creation . . . than the fact of copying it after the greatest of all creations, the cosmogony."[70] In an attempt to see his confused world as an orderly system, in search of some surer foundation for his own creative efforts, Mack labors through *The Encyclopedia of Philosophy* and Carl Sagan's *Cosmos*. Finally, though, Mack's skepticism overwhelms his need for assurance, and he refuses to believe what he reads. Just as Mack's tabletop is carefully finished but still incomplete, his reading is extensive but disturbingly inconclusive. The curious variety of his reading material (from books on astrophysics to the *Old Farmer's Almanac*) may actually be an index to his confusion. Among his list of books read are *Rage of Angels* and *The Clowns of God*. Such titles serve as ironic indictments of Mack's failure to construct a peaceful and harmonious vision.

Although Mack is much less addicted to television than many other Mason characters, he occasionally looks up from his books toward the tube for possible revelation. Michael Marsden comments that the television set has gradually taken on the role of a household god and, especially in its omnipresence, exhibits many quasi-divine qualities. As its divine bounty, television offers "a restructured, reformulated world in which the senseless makes sense" and where closure and resolution occur with predictable regularity.[71] If television serves up distinct 30-minute segments of order, it still displays serial disorder. In watching pudding commercials, football games, and *The Incredible Hulk*, Mack experiences quick shifts from one advertisement to another, from a particular program to one that is radically different. The essence of television is a rapidly changing pattern of tiny luminescent dots, and the flickering image on a screen at any given moment may have no connection to the image there a split second earlier or later. Thus, despite its omnipresence, television offers Mack no real coherence.

By making his imaginative card table, Mack encourages Mary Lou's social activity as a Rook player even if he cannot make himself fit into the composition. In her gregarious behavior Mary Lou is both a foil to Mack and a bridge connecting people and disparate elements of the culture. At one point she attends an R-rated movie, accompanied by both her youngest daughter Judy and an elderly member of the Rook group. Even in the food she serves, Mary Lou manages to create ad hoc harmony between the old-fashioned and the new. When Judy appears unexpectedly one evening with a hot pizza, Mary Lou calmly integrates it into her previous menu of corn and green beans.

Even though Mary Lou is not an artist or a student of cosmology, she understands intuitively how certain principles from Judy's physics textbook apply to her own family. On one of her visits home from college, Judy explains to her bewildered parents that photons are minute particles that disappear whenever someone begins to look for them. In fact, such particles simply don't exist "except in a group" (*S*, 27). Mary Lou reflects that the members of her family are scattering, and she fears that "if you break up a group, the individuals could disappear out of existence" (29). Her brother Ed took off for the West nine years earlier, and her only contact with him has been one recent phone call. In his isolation Ed ceases to be real to Mary Lou, and Ed's own comment that he is too thin to cast a shadow indicates that he has become a phantom. Mack is an agoraphobe rather than a wanderer, but Mary Lou is afraid that he "is disappearing," just like Ed, because he is "disconnected from everybody" (29). Mary Lou has some sensory evidence of her husband's continuing existence—the sounds of power tools and swearing from his shop—but she has difficulty discovering any reality behind these isolated phenomena. The real Mack is becoming as elusive as a photon.

Mary Lou repeatedly invites Mack to join the convivial Rookers, but he just as frequently declines. Having failed either to create or to perceive a coherent pattern in life, Mack has difficulty establishing even a tenuous connection with other people. During one evening of cards at his own home, he avoids the players but moves uneasily between watching *The Incredible Hulk* on television and repeatedly dialing the time-and-temperature number. On television he follows the adventures of a bizarre outsider; on the telephone he can pretend that he is involved with people without ever having to speak. Mack delights in the rapidly falling temperatures and hopes for snow so he won't have to leave the house. As the story ends he stands "in a frozen pose" (*S*, 33) with the telephone receiver in his hand. In this silent, deathlike stasis Mack approaches the condition that he fears most. In his misguided attempts to evade aging and death, he has become prematurely and morbidly old. As Leslie White observes, he simply "ices over" (White, 72). Ironically, the creative artist has transformed himself into static art object. Here Mack closely resembles his carefully fitted but sadly incomplete table-top, insulated from the world by clear polyurethane.

"Old Things" (1981)

Cleo Watkins, the main character of "Old Things," begins the story by proclaiming to her friend Rita Jean, "I'm still in one piece" (*S*, 75). In view of the general fragmentation and discord that surround her, maintaining this singular status is no small accomplishment. This story displays numerous examples of old things ripping apart and considers several strategies for holding them together. Foremost among these strategies is Cleo's humble craft as a seamstress. In its root sense "craft" means "strength," and Cleo must use all the powers at her disposal to combat incipient chaos.

The generic noun in Mason's title has many possible referents. One obvious category of old things includes the decrepit antiques that Cleo cleared from her house and that her daughter, Linda, now seeks out at the stockyard trade day. For her grandchildren Cleo is herself another example of an old thing, even though at 52 she should be in the prime of her life. In a more abstract sense Mason's title could refer to old institutions like marriage or traditional values like fidelity, neither of which has aged gracefully in this story.

A basic principle of thermodynamics asserts that, since all matter tends to lose available energy as time passes, the total entropy of the universe is continually increasing. In this story the inevitable passage of time brings both aging and disintegration on several levels. On a purely physical level Cleo works to keep her house in shape, but her resident grandchildren, Tammy and Davey, soon make it look as if a cyclone has struck. Amid the clutter of toys and clothing, Cleo looks longingly at a mail-order catalog that offers closet accessories to help organize one's possessions. Later she collects scattered pictures belonging to her granddaughter, unsuccessfully hunts a box that will hold them, and ultimately buys an album with a neat plastic pocket for each picture.

Such disorder of physical things disturbs Cleo because it is an obvious correlative of the social fragmentation that has disrupted her life. Cleo's daughter and grandchildren have moved into her house because Linda is separated from her husband. Now she leaves her children with Cleo and goes off to concerts in Paducah. In addition to this disintegration of her own family, Cleo sees abundant evidence that the phenomenon is widespread. A divorced acquaintance lets her husband keep their children, and Cleo marvels that any mother could abandon her kids and then go "gallivanting around" (*S*, 80).

In Cleo's brief but not so incidental references to photographs, Mason recalls an image important in several other stories (most notably, "Nancy Culpepper," "Lying Doggo," and "Coyotes"). Here the quality of the photographs that disturbs Cleo is their randomness. Snapped by Tammy's aptly named Minute Maker camera and then strewn haphazardly throughout the house, the photographs are emblematic of the discontinuity Cleo sees all around her. According to Susan Sontag, "photography reinforces a nominalist view of reality as consisting of small units of an apparently infinite number" (Sontag, 22). "Minute" in the name of Tammy's camera probably refers to a unit of time, but it could just as well denote minimal size. By presenting an endless series "of unrelated freestanding particles," the camera makes the world atomic and denies interconnectedness (23).

In encouraging Tammy to arrange her snapshots in an album, Cleo seeks an ordering frame and a thread of continuity for such atomic particles. Her own family photograph album is the only remaining memento of her dead husband, and late one night Cleo retreats to the album in search of reassurance. Even here, though, the aging photographs are coming loose from the pages and confronting each other "at crazy angles" (*S*, 89). The carefully imposed order has become tenuous, the frames on segments of reality askew. Nevertheless, photographs of lost family members remain as totems, and the act of poring through the album is elevated to ritual.

Sontag notes that the elaborate rites of taking and preserving family pictures developed in America at about the same time as the extended family was diminishing to the nuclear family. Ironically, then, photographs serve "to memorialize, to restate symbolically, the imperiled continuity and vanishing extendedness of family life" (Sontag, 9). The random photographs in "Old Things" are manifestations of an even greater irony. Tammy cannot take a picture of her absent father, and instead of photographing her actual mother, she snaps the blurred image of a woman on the television screen, says it is like her mama, and inserts it in the family album. Such confused images document the further decline of the family into ad hoc intergenerational groupings. The devolution has progressed from extended through nuclear to highly particular.

If still photographs provide commentary on social disintegration, the rapidly changing images on the television screen are even more eloquent. Throughout the story Mason skillfully uses references to television programs to document relationships falling apart. In the daily television log, disturbing reports on *Today* (portraying men as single parents) give way to questionable jokes on *Tonight* (reminding Cleo that Johnny Carson has been divorced twice), which eventually fade into even more alarming developments on *Tomorrow* (depictions of alcoholism among teenagers). While the program names in this sequence indicate the steady march of time, the program contents provide evidence of increasingly grave problems.

Beset by physical disorder and social fragmentation, Cleo also experiences corresponding semantic disjunctions. She hears a barrage of sounds but finds them largely devoid of meaning. Instead of creating order from chaos (as they presumably did at the beginning of time), words are now just a further manifestation of the general disorder. When Cleo enters her house after a shopping trip, the sounds of a violent television program, the words of a song blaring from the radio, and Tammy's half of a telephone conversation all compete for her attention. To her friend on the phone Tammy exclaims: "What do you mean, what do I mean? Oh, you know what I mean" (*S*, 77). For Cleo, however, such "patter . . . is meaningless" (77). The medium of Mason's own art is language, but here she uses disembodied words to display semantic chaos. Like lines from an absurdist drama, such snippets of dialogue communicate not sense but its perplexing absence. Later Cleo argues with Linda while in the background Tammy argues with Davey. With claims and counterclaims flying freely about, "the racket is losing its definition" (88). Cleo finds it difficult to distinguish individual sounds, and the merged voices are "something like a prolonged, steady snore" (88). In such a situation signification degenerates to white noise; logos becomes logorrhea.

In the face of all this physical, social, and linguistic disintegration, the characters in "Old Things" must devise personal strategies for coping. In commenting on the story "Residents and Transients," Mason has stated that a major theme in *Shiloh and Other Stories* is the tension between holding stubbornly to the past and moving headlong into the future (Wendy Smith, 425). Such a dilemma is obviously central to "Old Things" and defines the debate between Cleo and Linda.

During times of rapid change, people's attitudes toward the old and the new may be curiously ambivalent. Linda, for example, declares the value of "keeping up with the times" (*S*, 87) and relishes her freedom from former social restraints. At the same time she reverts to the old-fashioned in her praise of Duke Ellington's band and in her enthusiastic purchases of antiques. Jeff Ferrell has noted that many consumer products (e.g., furniture and clothing) go through four stages of degradation and rehabilitation—new, old, used, and vintage.[72] Linda disavows old things but begins to value them again once they have progressed to the status of vintage. Ironically, Linda extols the new while she tries to rejuvenate an antique rocking chair. Her search for "old-timey stuff" (*S*, 87) no doubt reflects a more inclusive longing for the security of the past, like that of Leroy in "Shiloh" or Liz in "Sorghum." In particular, her efforts to find a mate for the antique rocker suggest regret at the breakup of her marriage and nostalgia for the old paired relationship.

Cleo's balancing of the old against the new is equally complex. She insists that she "doesn't want to live in the past" (*S*, 76), and soon after her husband's death she disposes of many old things and moves into a new house. Nevertheless, Cleo is a professional seamstress who sews with such care that she seems to be trying to repair the torn fabric of society. Like other meticulous craftspeople (e.g., Leroy in "Shiloh" or Mack in "The Rookers"), she aims to construct something lasting that will survive the ravages of time. Like the social paradigms all around, her paper patterns are "flimsy" (77) and easily torn, but she pins them to the fabric with utmost care. To insure that her garments will resist rips and tears, she "whips the facings" (85) and makes "double seams" (77). As an additional measure of security, she constructs "pockets with flaps" (77). Cleo knows, of course, that all things age and decay, but her ritualistic sewing may in some small way delay this process.

Like Mrs. Sisson in "Drawing Names" and Lila in *Spence + Lila*, Cleo pursues the traditional woman's art associated with literary heroines since the time of Penelope. Her adherence to the old craft demonstrates her sharp difference with her daughter and her inclination to address contemporary problems through time-honored means. In a seventeenth-century poem like Edward Taylor's "Huswifery," the needle arts could provide a powerful metaphor for harmony and divine order, but now such activities may seem archaic and ineffectual. Cleo's art provides only a temporary stay against the general unraveling of society.

Cleo ends the story with a nostalgic tribute to the past and another simple act of ritualistic creation. Like her "antique-crazy" daughter (*S*, 76) she goes to trade day and discovers an old whatnot identical to one that belonged to her husband. This whatnot has labeled boxes, like tiny books on a shelf, to hold "Mending Tape, Gummed Patches, Rubber Bands" (92), and other small items. Each box also has part of a picture on its spine, and arranged in their proper order they present an old-fashioned scene of a train running through a meadow. Despite her alleged aversion to antiques, Cleo buys this piece and promptly places the boxes in the correct sequence. Like the new items she admires in the mail-order catalog, this particular old thing probably appeals to her because it is a tool for creating order. Furthermore, the labels on the tiny boxes promise assistance in mending, patching, and binding together, and such actions—closely akin to those in her sewing—are sorely needed all around her. With its pleasant pastoral scene, the old whatnot also provides Cleo a consoling visual image of continuity between the past and the future. As she rearranges the components of the picture to make everything fit, she also creates a more pleasing picture of her own family. She imagines Linda and her husband driving the train together, Tammy and Davey riding patiently along, and herself following carefree in the tiny caboose. In perfect harmony "they all wave at the future and smile perfect smiles" (93). Cleo's vision is an improbable fantasy, but it offers a temporary refuge from disorder as she grows older. In the picture on this antique whatnot, as in her sewing, she discovers momentary solace. In the whatnot's neat compartments, as in her careful stitching, she finds reinforcement of her efforts to order and mend a fractured world.

"Marita" (1988)

The central character of "Marita" resembles Samantha Hughes in Mason's novel *In Country*. Both Sam and Marita are recent high school graduates with minimal plans for the future. Both girls grow up without fathers, develop tangled relationships with their mothers, and remain confused about their own identities. Sam counsels her best friend, who fears that she may be pregnant. Marita actually becomes pregnant during her first semester of college, drops out of school, and has an abortion. In search of her identity, Sam studies old letters from her father (who was killed in Vietnam) and makes a pilgrimage to the Vietnam Veterans Memorial in Washington. Marita also struggles to define herself, but her efforts are more erratic and inconclusive.

This story contains no authentic artists, but it does show the problems that result from a confusion of biological reproduction with artistic creation. In high school Marita wanted to become an artist, and her mother loved to draw before she became too exhausted for creative activity. Now, as the daughter of divorced parents, Marita aspires to create but becomes instead a living medium for her mother's frustrated attempts at artistic expression. First Sue Ellen creates an exotic name for her daughter. A fusion of the names of two aunts, Mary and Rita, it suggests a prefabricated identity imposed on Marita at birth. When Marita is only 10 years old, Sue Ellen begins to adorn the child with makeup in an attempt to see what she will look like as a grown woman. By creating a new face for Marita, she hopes to mold her emerging identity. Sue Ellen thinks the name Marita sounds Spanish, and at one point she dresses her daughter for a party in the costume of a Spanish fan dancer. Such a flamboyant outfit represents an artificial role that Marita must escape before she can discover herself, but she cannot do so gracefully. Despite Sue Ellen's grand creative efforts the costume is, in fact, a bathetic failure. When Marita's date throws up in her lap, she has to rake out the vomit with her fan.

Due to Sue Ellen's artistic efforts and the genes she shares with Marita, mother and daughter are actually so much alike that people mistake them for sisters. They share the same facial features, and with matching honey-beige skin tones, they can even wear the same foundation. Marita resists this homogeneity because she fears being absorbed into her mother. She feels so derivative and diminished that she compares herself and her cats to the tiny Borrowers in a series of popular children's books. With a borrowed identity Marita lives unseen and unheard in a mysterious substratum comparable to that of the children's story. The real world is contiguous, but she cannot break through to it. Far from being an accomplished artist in her own right, Marita sees herself as a literary character—the product of another, more powerful creator.

Mason further dramatizes the tug-of-war between mother and daughter through the story's point of view. Few of Mason's stories use multiple points of view, but this one shifts frequently between Marita's first-person comments and third-person accounts of Sue Ellen's thoughts and actions. Marita begins the story, but her subjective musings soon give way to authoritative statements about and by her mother. Just as Sue Ellen dominates Marita, the highly privileged third-person narrative regularly displaces the young woman's tentative voice. At one point Sue Ellen wants to read her daughter's mind so she can "revise it and stick in some things Marita needed to think about" (*LL*, 56). Apparently Sue Ellen wants to be more than a makeup artist and costumer. In effect she would like to become a quasi-literary creator—the omniscient narrator of Marita's own story.

Marita suffers from an adolescent version of anxiety of influence—the bane of any aspiring artist. As Harold Bloom notes, all creators must "wrestle with their precursors" in order to "clear imaginative space for themselves."[73] Frequently denied a voice, Marita struggles to stake out her territory—any arena of creative activity or knowledge that her loving but misguided mother will not invade. In a typically adolescent fashion she jumps quickly from one passing interest to another. One week she explores world religions, then she develops a passion for science-fiction novels, and soon after that she begins to follow the stock market.

Among Marita's passing interests, the most serious is maternity. Mason's novel *Feather Crowns* portrays the powerful effects of the birth (and death) of quintuplets. The force of maternity in this story is not nearly so dramatic and intense, but in her unborn child Marita sees, at least temporarily, one possibility for creating autonomy for herself. Marita believes that her own mother is living her life through her daughter. Following Sue Ellen's example, Marita apparently believes that she can escape childhood by becoming a mother herself—that she can create a new identity by making a baby. Thus, in attempting to escape the influence of her mother, she simply replicates Sue Ellen's error. Marita suffers from the malady that Adrienne Rich calls matrophobia. Marita's personality seems "dangerously to blur and overlap" with that of her mother. In her desire "to become individuated and free," to "know where mother ends and daughter begins," Marita pursues an extreme course (Rich, 236).

Marita's highly questionable assumptions recall a distorted lesson from high school home economics. Students in that class were required to create and care for flour babies—dolls made of stretch fabric filled with 10 pounds of flour. Since students had to take these dolls everywhere, they were intended to teach the permanent responsibilities of having a baby. For some girls in the class, however, the plan backfired. They loved their dolls so much that they actually wanted to become pregnant and bring their flour babies to life.

Marita's pregnancy is not deliberate, but it does illustrate her desire to create something all her own. The high school home economics class provided a very limited opportunity for artistic expression. To satisfy class requirements, Marita created not one but two distinctive flour babies. The first one had "warty ears and a big nose and a blue birthmark" (*LL*, 67), but when its flour began to leak Marita had to construct a replacement. This time she made a prettier doll with button eyes and red yarn hair. Just as Sue Ellen experimented with makeup on Marita, the flour babies allowed Marita the opportunity to shape and decorate as she pleased, and the unorthodox results displayed her urge to escape both artistic and social conventions. As she begins to create a real baby, she decides to go to beauty school so she can be the one who applies makeup and executes makeovers. In resisting her mother's advice to have an abortion, Marita proclaims, "I don't want anybody sticking a vacuum cleaner up me" (60). In this brief but vehement objection she expresses her fear that the abortion procedure will leave her an empty shell. Without her baby and the grand hopes attached to it, she may again become a void. Marita's resistance to the abortion is perfunctory, however, because even she sees that her hopes are unrealistic.

The termination of her pregnancy reminds Marita of the end of the flour baby project when she bashed her doll against the school wall and then "ran free—like a young dog after a flying Frisbee, like someone in love" (*LL*, 67). Such images suggest glorious abandon, but Marita does note that she tracked flour down the sidewalk as she ran. If such traces of the past marked her path, her freedom was hardly complete. In her present situation Marita is ready to return to college and continue her search for autonomy. In doing so, however, she will carry with her the influence of an assertive mother and the pain of an accidental pregnancy. In forging a new identity, Marita must deal with these important details of her personal history rather than attempting to leave them behind like a bashed flour baby. Marita has experienced pregnancy, but she has not gone on to become a parent. She has exercised artistic aspirations but has created nothing that she can value. On the verge of maturity, she is pulled back to remain (at least for a time) a child still highly dependent upon her mother.

"Still Life with Watermelon" (1982)

Of all collected Mason stories, "Still Life with Watermelon" is the most chaotic. Relationships of characters are disjointed, and their spurts of action are erratic. Despite its title the lives displayed in this story are anything but still. Indeed, the characters here are like bumper cars that suddenly jerk into motion, collide with other vehicles, and carom off in totally unexpected directions.

Throughout the story relationships are so tenuous and temporary that the reader may need a flowchart to follow the complex permutations. At the beginning Louise Milsap shares her house with Peggy Wilson because the husbands of both women have temporarily deserted them. Tom Milsap has abandoned his contracting business and headed for Texas with his former employee, Jim Yates, to become a "born-again cowboy" (*S*, 61). These two men work briefly on a ranch owned by Jim's uncle until Jim (whom Peggy suspects to be homosexual) runs even farther away to Mexico with an unnamed woman. Peggy and her husband Jerry (a.k.a. Flathead) formerly lived in Paducah in the home of an eccentric art collector named Herman Priddle. Three nights a week Eddy Gail Moses also resided there as Herman's mistress and cook. Eventually Eddy linked up with Jerry, and the two went to live with Eddy's father. For a time Peggy continued to live with Herman, but after being frightened by the "lecherous grin" (64) of a sliced watermelon in one of Herman's paintings, she moved in with Louise. In due course Jerry leaves Eddy and reclaims Peggy just in time for Tom to return to Louise. Meanwhile Herman goes to the hospital with a stroke, and a niece takes over his grand house.

Mason's plot is hyperbolic, but this mimetic strategy raises important questions. To what extent does her chaotic story line parallel events of a confused world? To what degree do the dysfunctional relationships of her characters mimic those of real people? Mason further explores the question of how art imitates life by making her main character an aspiring artist. Amid so many erratic travelers Louise is the only character who remains fixed in one place, who attempts to create order rather than pursue it along some faint trail. Laid off from her job at Kroger's, she decides to paint dozens of watermelon pictures, which she thinks she can sell to Herman. As a visual artist her two main problems are verisimilitude, capturing on canvas the reality of a watermelon, and composition, placing the watermelon in a cohesive arrangement with other objects. Both of these aesthetic problems parallel the larger problems of Mason's characters.

Louise's early paintings are obvious failures as representational art. Her first watermelon looks "like a dark-green basketball floating on an algae-covered pond" (*S*, 60). Other early pictures "appear to be optical illusions—watermelons disappearing like black holes into vacant skies" (67). Largely by chance Louise depicts on these canvases not the watermelon itself but rather the elusiveness of the image she seeks. While her watermelons seem to disappear, the vision of order that she tries to capture is equally evasive.

Just as Louise has difficulty producing realistic images of watermelons, most of the other characters in this story are confused travelers unable to form accurate visions of the world around them. Fantasies displace reality and motivate unlikely aspirations. Tom, for example, thinks he can be a cowboy even though he has never mounted a horse. As evidence of an equally loose grip on reality, Jim Yates acts as if he is continually playing the video game Space Invaders. Still another disoriented male, Jerry Wilson, runs off with an older woman because he wants to be babied and thus evade the problems of adulthood. Although Peggy has been abandoned, she persistently fantasizes that the telephone will ring at any moment with wonderful news, that Jerry will take her off to New Orleans on a dream vacation, that she will become fabulously wealthy.

An even more dramatic example of distorted vision is Herman Priddle's passion for collecting images of watermelons. This mania emerges in the winter of Herman's life after Eddy Gail has deserted him. At this point Herman haunts antique shops, pores through catalogs, and even places advertisements in trade papers in search of more watermelon pictures. In due time his collection includes drawings, watercolors, oil paintings, tapestries, needlepoint chair covers, and china plates. The juicy, brightly colored watermelon evokes visions of summertime and easy living. For Herman in his old age, this elusive fruit has become an icon for the idyllic past. Having lost the substance of youth, he clings to a poor facsimile, and in doing so he draws Louise into his flimsy dream. Herman's delusive hopes fuel her equally unrealistic expectations. Although she has never met Herman, he becomes her "watermelon man" (*S*, 68) who will pay fantastic prices for her pictures.

In the process of painting watermelons, Louise gradually learns that the artistic problems of verisimilitude and composition are closely connected. All too often her images are not credible because the backgrounds don't suit the melons. She tries painting watermelons with apples and grapes, but discrepancies in size make everything "appear odd and unnatural" (*S*, 60). With limited success she paints watermelons with candles, watermelons with clouds, even watermelons with wire pliers. In one painting a "watermelon on a flowered tablecloth resembles a blimp that has landed in a petunia bed" (67).

Although Louise's paintings seldom fool the eye, she does learn that appropriate composition enhances verisimilitude. In like manner characters in this story who clarify their confused relationships can hope to achieve more accurate perceptions of reality. Although relationships at the start of the story are as surreal as Louise's combinations of fruit and tools, some eventually become more harmonious. Tom, for example, returns to Louise intent on straightening out their marriage, getting a small business loan, and rebuilding his contracting company. Instead of wandering the trail as a lonely cowboy, he will work again in construction—assembling parts to form a harmonious whole.

After Tom returns, Louise sees their life together as a painting in progress. As he comes up the walk, "his face is in shadow" and "his features aren't painted in" (*S*, 73–74). Behind him is a vacant lot full of weeds, and in this familiar background Louise notices for the first time that subtle colors like amber, yellow, and deep purple begin to leap out at her. Although Louise failed as a painter of watermelons, she displays in this scene the vision of a true artist. In the shadowy face of a husband who deserted her, she sees the potential for newly defined features. In the mundane field of weeds, she discovers vibrant colors that she previously overlooked. Since the background of this unfinished painting is an "empty field . . . dancing with light" (74), the artist can devise an appropriate composition to complement the central figures. Even if her watermelon still lifes were unsuccessful, Louise can still create a more harmonious and comprehensive landscape with the person she loves in the central foreground.

In "Still Life with Watermelon," then, several problems of composition dovetail neatly. As she creates the entire text, Mason experiments with strategies of literary composition. Within this text another artist explores the problems of composing a credible still life. Finally, all the characters in the story must consider methods of integrating self with society and creating a convincing whole out of many disparate parts.

"Coyotes" (1988)

Indigenous to western North America, the coyote has in recent years expanded its domain to include most of the continent. This adaptable species thrives in highly diverse environments and on diets ranging from sheep and cattle to berries and garbage. In some cases coyotes have encroached upon densely populated areas, and one even took up residence in New York City's Central Park. In her story entitled "Coyotes," Mason notes the recent incursion of the species into Kentucky, and she uses certain qualities of the wild animal to reflect upon the dilemma of her human characters. These humans find themselves in strangely confused situations that require all their resources to adapt and survive. Some, like the young protagonist Cobb and his girlfriend, Lynnette, are able to cope and flourish. Others, like Lynnette's mother, become severely disturbed and helpless.

Like the jumbled environments of the coyote, human living spaces in this story reflect disorder. In particular, the home of Cobb's mother and stepfather is a truly bizarre ecosystem and an aesthetic disaster area. All around the living room, Early American furniture clashes with sleek modern pieces, and on the walls needlepoint images of castles compete with paintings of the Amish in their buggies. Obviously Cobb's mother displays no skill in artistic composition, but such interior decoration is more than an offense against good taste. By labeling the house "a case study" (*LL*, 172), Cobb implies that the aesthetic disharmony of the place parallels the emotional and spiritual confusion of its inhabitants. Some years earlier his father ran off to Chicago with another woman, leaving his mother to find a second husband. For Cobb this new stepfather is like an especially discordant note in the decor.

A young adult living in his own apartment, Cobb is much more focused and mature than Steve in "Midnight Magic," but he cannot really escape environmental confusion by moving away from home. His live-in girlfriend brings home from her job abundant evidence of the world's disorder. Lynnette works at a film-developing company where photographs roll off an assembly line for her to inspect and package. In other Mason stories like "Nancy Culpepper" and "Lying Doggo," individual pictures are important metaphors. In this story the content of a specific photograph is less significant than the strangeness of certain photograph sequences. The order of exposures on rolls of film and the assembly line itself establish a sequence of images, but this order is somewhat arbitrary. As Lynnette examines the steady stream of prints, she feels compelled to interpret and make connections among them. To create order in this disturbing randomness, she becomes a literary artist fabricating stories that explain the odd groupings of images. Susan Sontag asserts that any photograph is "a potential object of fascination" with "multiple meanings." It says to the viewer: "There is the surface. Now think—rather feel, intuit—what is beyond it, what the reality must be like if it looks this way." Although photographs cannot in themselves provide explanations, they are "inexhaustible invitations to deduction, speculation, and fantasy" (Sontag, 23).

One batch of photographs at Lynnette's company, apparently from a Florida vacation, consists of pictures of tree bark and roots, a small stucco house, cars in parking lots, and a boardwalk trail through woods. Lynnette's explanatory narrative posits an older couple who return to their former home and find the shrubs towering like monsters, the house occupied by people who chase them away, and the landscape overrun with cars. Eventually they go to the woods where the wife was once raped, and there she loses her wedding ring through a crack in the boardwalk. In searching for meaning beneath the surface phenomena, Lynnette creates a surreal tale of change and tragic loss. Her connect-the-dots story uncovers but orders the horrors hidden away in the interstices of life.

At the heart of Lynnette's fiction is the postmodernist technique of remotivation—boldly appropriating old signs or images and placing them in new contexts where they assume different meanings. This century's widespread mechanical reproduction of art and literature has led to a massive increase in the number of available signs and "an uncontrollable multiplication of their possible contextualizations."[74] Such is particularly the case with easily reproduced photographs. In the postmodern era photography swiftly and succinctly isolates "fragments of the world" and makes them "available for endless reframings" (Ray, 135). On the assembly line, when Lynnette confronts individual images that are frightening or merely puzzling, she creates an ad hoc order by redirecting fragments of her world into new contexts. Edward Ball compares such creative remotivations to hijackings since the artist assumes control of a vehicle and diverts it to a new site.[75]

Even when Lynnette's postmodern stories are grim, they provide some insulation from the painful reality of her work. On her assembly line, pictures of people brandishing weapons are juxtaposed with home-made pornographic images. Pictures of drownings and gunshot victims (from rolls of film brought in by the police) get "all mixed in with vacations and children" (*LL*, 173). Like Donald in "Big Bertha Stories," Lynnette uses her creative powers to keep such real-life horrors at bay. As she quickly slips groups of photographs into envelopes, she just as efficiently encloses the offending images within some comprehensive narrative. Her steady stream of fictions, filled with remotivated images, corresponds to her compulsive running. Lynnette is never still and even wants to have sex during the most frightening parts of a movie she watches with Cobb on television. Thus, the frenetic pace of her body matches that of her imagination.

In her spontaneous fictions, in her running six to eight miles a day, in her desire for love during a horror movie, Lynnette is trying to elude one haunting image from her past—that of her mentally ill mother. If Lynnette's need to create order through art is pronounced, her mother's need for order is all-consuming. Lynnette's creative efforts are energizing, those of her mother debilitating. Faced with an unfaithful husband, she at first spends her days "pasting up wallpaper or arranging artificial flowers" (*LL*, 178). When these surface measures fail to satisfy her deeper needs, she begins obsessively to count things around the house and ultimately tries to arrange an orderly death by means of a Valium overdose.

Like the adaptable coyote, Cobb remains undaunted by the eccentricities of Lynnette and her family. In fact, he delights in her fertile imagination—her remarkable ability to "look at something and have a take on it. Not just take it for granted" (*LL*, 171). Cobb met Lynnette at her workplace when he picked up some pictures from a very conventional Florida vacation. Realizing that she had examined his photographs, he too had an immediate epiphany about the triteness of his experiences. Cobb perceived the reality of his own life only after it was portrayed in a series of clichéd photographs and silently evaluated by Lynnette. Months later her artistic creativity continues to bring out the "fresh and unexpected in him" (*LL*, 164), and he even begins on a lesser scale to mimic her efforts to create order through story making. When he overhears snatches of conversation at Wal-Mart, he tries to invent connections and explanations of these verbal snapshots as Lynnette does with her photographs.

Just as the coyote boldly extends its territory, at the end of this story Cobb and Lynnette venture into an uncertain future. Cobb's brother has recently sighted a coyote coming into his own yard to stalk a trompe l'oeil wind sock shaped like a goose. This wind sock looks so real that it also fools Cobb temporarily. If the wily coyote cannot always perceive his new environment accurately, the human characters may certainly stumble and falter as they enter new stages in life and explore new terrain. Cobb is concerned that he doesn't understand Lynnette—that he will mess up their relationship without even knowing it. Fearful that she may become like her mother, Lynnette expresses reservations about their marriage. Such doubts are themselves good insurance against self-deception. The hyperrealistic wind sock shows that Cobb and Lynnette may at times confuse art and reality and thus view their world incorrectly. More often, however, they can use their ad hoc art to scrutinize and better comprehend its oddities. Fully aware of life's complications but strongly committed to confronting them, Cobb and Lynnette display greater resources for success than most other young couples in Mason's stories. Like the coyote they should not merely cope but prevail.

"Big Bertha Stories" (1985)

Again and again the characters in Mason's stories have difficulties in "retaining identity and integrity in the face of change" (Wilhelm, 1987, 272). In "Big Bertha Stories" the specific shock that threatens identity is not divorce or job loss but combat in Vietnam. Mason wrote this story while she was working on the novel *In Country*, and the two works develop similar characters and themes. Both examine the residual effects of war—the domestic aftermath of American involvement in Southeast Asia. In both works soldiers search for the way back home, and their odysseys, stripped of all heroism, are even more trying than that of Ulysses.

In "Big Bertha Stories" the protagonist is, like Mason, a storyteller, but his tales are chaotic and inconclusive. Mason's story is itself a metafictional frame focusing on the painful alienation of a Vietnam veteran called Donald. Within this frame the disjointed stories Donald tells his young son are the most prominent displays of his psychological dislocation. The stories invented by Lynnette in "Coyotes" provide a template for arranging the disturbingly random images that bombard her. Donald's stories are far more ambitious but far less successful. Failing to cohere, they usually begin with bluster but diminish to an enigmatic whimper.

Promptly after his physical return from the war, Donald takes a job in a lumberyard, marries, and fathers a son. This interlude of apparent normalcy soon ends, however, when horrible memories of war overwhelm him and call him back to psychological combat. Moving from construction back to destruction, Donald deliberately sabotages his job and leaves his family to work in the strip mines of remote Muhlenberg County. In operating a massive earth-moving machine, Donald reverts to a symbolic war zone. Just as the machinery of combat despoiled the Vietnamese countryside, Donald's earthmover destroys the land in its path. Mason's story never displays this faraway destruction but focuses instead on Donald's sporadic and increasingly turbulent visits back home. Because Donald has never found his way back from the emotional chaos of battle, he is trapped in a cycle of incomplete and unsatisfactory returns to his family. During each visit he is less like a husband or father than like "an absentee landlord" (*LL*, 116) who never really belongs.

At home Donald suffers strange dreams that mirror the lasting effects of prior trauma. As evidence of his alienation and anger at the country that sent him off to Vietnam, he dreams of fleeing to Cuba on a hijacked plane. In response to feelings of helplessness and vulnerability, he dreams about protecting his house with strings of barbed wire. One other persistent dream focuses on a mysterious lost doll, which may symbolize the innocence of Donald's youth, sadly misplaced somewhere in the jungles of Southeast Asia.

Such dreams are haunting protonarratives—fragmentary accounts of tragic loss dictated by Donald's subconscious. His bizarre stories about Big Bertha are the more extended, public narratives of a disturbed mind. Ostensibly Big Bertha is a giant strip-mining machine from Muhlenberg County, but her symbolic significance exceeds even her physical size. Like a cartoon superhero she can "straddle a four-lane highway" (*LL*, 120) or stand as tall as a skyscraper. Like the protagonist of a frontier tall tale, she generates a tornado whenever she belches. Truly protean in form, she becomes at various points in the tortured fictions a trainer of snakes that win 500-mile races, a fat woman who sings the blues, and "a female version of Paul Bunyan" (117). The unfathomable complexity of Donald's fictional heroine reflects the inner confusion of her creator. The relentless inflation of Big Bertha's alleged powers is an indication of his increasing desperation. In formulating such elaborate fictions, Donald is akin to the protagonist of Tim O'Brien's *Going After Cacciato*. In that novel "Paul's solution to the horror and chaos of memory is to substitute for a possibility that happened—the 'real' war—one that did not."[76] Both in its motive and its grandiose scale, Paul's fantasy of an overland escape from Vietnam to Paris parallels Donald's adventures of Big Bertha.

One of Donald's most complicated stories, "Big Bertha and the Neutron Bomb," is set in California, where Big Bertha takes a surfing holiday. At first this setting is as idyllic as the big rock candy mountain: "On the beach, corn dogs and snow cones are free and the surfboards turn into dolphins" (*LL*, 119). With an abrupt shift of tone, however, a neutron bomb appears and everyone except the superheroine suddenly "keels over dead" (119). The story boldly asserts that Big Bertha remains immune to the bomb, but (as evidence of his own vulnerability) Donald simply ends his narrative without ever developing this claim. A later story links Big Bertha with a rock-and-roll band—another icon, like the surfers, of joyous freedom. Unfortunately, this band presents a concert at a site that was once a toxic-waste dump, and in later travels they accidentally spread contamination all over the country. As coded images Donald's toxic-waste site recalls the battlefields of Vietnam, and the subsequent contamination suggests the virulent consequences of the war within the United States. In spite of Big Bertha's celebrated powers, at the end of this long but confusing story her "solution to the problem is not at all clear" (126).

Since the Big Bertha stories are veiled accounts of Donald's experiences in Vietnam, they typically begin in playful innocence but soon disintegrate into confusion or horror. By continually inflating Big Bertha's powers, Donald tries to make her a savior of mythical proportions. Unfortunately, this jerry-built deus ex machina repeatedly fails to solve the problems at hand. In fact, as Donald's abortive myths become increasingly disjointed, his central character becomes more remote and menacing.

When Donald can filter out memories of destruction, he actually recalls Vietnam as "the most beautiful place in the world"—a spot so lush "you'd have thought you were in paradise" (*LL,* 130). Paired with a childlike Vietnamese girlfriend, he enjoyed a taste of Eden until combat blew it apart. Donald's myths merge the horrible with the idyllic because he experienced just such a confusing mixture in Vietnam. There the hellish repeatedly infused and overwhelmed the Edenic. Now, just as Donald is a seeker of the pastoral who has been expelled from the garden and a traveler who cannot make it all the way home, he is also a narrator who cannot bring any of his stories to a satisfactory conclusion. His stories falter and break off because he cannot sustain hope when his memories are seared with horrors.

Donald's work in the coal fields and his cycle of unsatisfactory returns to his family eventually end when he agrees to enter a veterans' hospital. He goes there like an old man finally resigned to living in a rest home. Since Donald lost his youth in Vietnam and is therefore unable to fill the normal adult roles of husband and father, he jumps over the usual passages of life and becomes prematurely old. Riding calmly to the hospital, he composes one more Big Bertha story, but in this simple tale her actions are decidedly less flamboyant. Here Bertha does nothing more than take him on an ocean cruise bound for the South Seas. In evoking visions of a tropical paradise, this story may still reflect Donald's yearning for escape, but now the mechanism is hardly miraculous. Donald's mythopoeic powers have not proved equal to the demands of his tortured psyche. His fabulous Big Bertha is no longer a demigod but merely a cruise director or kindly nurse. In thus reducing the grandeur of his fictions, Donald may indicate his readiness to face the healing truth as he and other members of his therapy group swap down-to-earth stories of combat. In Mason's *In Country* a trip to the Vietnam Veterans Memorial in Washington suggests the potential for widespread healing of the national trauma. After his own experience at the wall, a central character, Emmett, proclaims that all of his fellow veterans are coming there someday. In "Big Bertha Stories" the hints of healing are less emphatic but still discernible.

Jerome Klinkowitz has criticized Mason's *In Country*, along with Jayne Anne Phillips's *Machine Dreams*, as outmoded fictive responses to the war in Vietnam. Both novels, he claims, "rely upon the hackneyed formula of 'family sagas.' " Thus, in their use of "unexamined social realism," they allegedly manage "to contextualize American actions in Vietnam without properly describing them, much less understanding the problems involved with structuring the void."[77] Whether or not such criticism of *In Country* is valid, Mason's strategy in "Big Bertha Stories" is decidedly more postmodern. This shorter account of the consequences of Vietnam does focus on episodes of family life, but more importantly it recognizes the difficulties inherent in formulating even a simple narrative. In dramatizing Donald's failed efforts as a storyteller, Mason acknowledges the difficulty of structuring content that refuses "to be pliably mimetic" (Klinkowitz, 147).

"Piano Fingers" (1988)

Unlike earlier stories in *Love Life*, "Piano Fingers" focuses on a conventional American family—two parents, a daughter, and a son all living together in a modest ranch-style house. Beset with debts and the threat of unemployment, the father of this family copes with past failures by driving around town and chasing unrealistic dreams for the future. Dean Harris is only 26 years old, but he has already experienced a series of jobs as well as a painful period of joblessness. After working at a filling station and a garage, he was employed briefly at the local tire plant. Ironically, all of these jobs were connected with travel, but each left him standing still at the side of the highway. Uncertain about his future, Dean remains immobilized—"suspended somewhere between childhood and old age, not knowing which direction he is facing" (*LL,* 84).

If Dean's grasp on the real world is tenuous and his ability to navigate in it limited, his fantasy life is rich and extensive. Just as Mary in "Residents and Transients" is a jaded traveler yearning for pastoral calm, Dean is a thwarted traveler (whose trips are mainly routine deliveries for the drugstore where he now works) aspiring to be an artist. When this story was originally published, it bore the revealing subtitle "Dreams in the Key of Being," and Mason has commented that the process of creating a literary work is like dreaming. In our dreams, she says, "we are telling ourselves stories, trying to create a meaning out of the chaos of memories and sensations floating around randomly in our heads" ("Creating"). Dean never manages to get his narratives onto paper, but the stories conjured up in his daydreams are expansive. While he watches dull television shows, Dean becomes a screenwriter mentally drafting superior scripts. In his television series the hero will be an average guy whose work driving a delivery van leads him to solve exotic crimes. Despite his "down-to-earth" qualities that "people can relate to" (*LL,* 82), this fearless crime solver will have a glamorous name (Ballinger), a flashy van (bright red with purple lettering), and an exotic locale (California).

The imaginary detective is, of course, a quixotic projection of Dean himself. After Dean makes a delivery from the drugstore to a local teacher, he becomes Ballinger and sees the teacher's house as the setting for a dramatic episode of his television show. He imagines that the teacher was a suspect in the murder of her lover back in Michigan. She fled to this obscure town and assumed a new identity to escape gossip. Although she is completely innocent, she knows the real killer and he is stalking her. In due time Ballinger rescues her from this villain and then "does wheelies around the courthouse square" in his "souped-up van" (*LL,* 90).

Just as Don Quixote jousts with windmills, Dean's fantasy scripted for television is far removed from actuality. In the cavorting of a souped-up van, Dean's art may indulge his desire for showy locomotion, but it fails, of course, to move him forward. Rather than informing real life, such art offers only escape from it. In reality Dean's venue for detection is not exotic California but a Kentucky cornfield recently transformed into a subdivision (still another chunk of the pastoral consumed by ruburban sprawl). Mason comments obliquely on the fraudulence of Dean's dream by noting that this particular development is named Birch

Hills even though it contains neither hills nor birches. Instead of a flashy van, he drives the drugstore car. Instead of living up to the exotic name Ballinger, Dean retains a name that is actually an ironic commentary on his failures. From the Latin *decanus*, meaning leader of 10, the name Dean implies a degree of power and status. In fact, this elevated name (like that of Leroy in "Shiloh") is sadly inconsistent with the character's lowly station.

In his scheme for a television show, Dean celebrates the long tradition of amateur detectives (from Auguste Dupin and Sherlock Holmes to Miss Marple and Jessica Fletcher) who outsmart the professionals by solving mysteries with elegance and grace. That Dean's art takes the form of a detective story is evidence of his desire to figure out life's puzzles, but it is also highly ironic. He cannot even begin to decipher the mysteries of his own existence or discern significant clues along his path. For Dean, life remains a show of illusion, and Mason uses the standard imagery of smoke and mirrors to emphasize this fact. At one point Dean notices wood smoke as it puffs out his chimney, drifts slowly across his yard, and disappears. In this insubstantial image "Dean sees himself when he leaves home in the morning to go out into the world" (*LL*, 89). Later, as he drives through town at night, he studies the lights reflected on the darkened windows of a bank. Here "some of the lights in the window are reflections of reflections, like a kaleidoscope of possibilities for his life" (96). In such a world Dean is not an artist creating order but the easily duped spectator at a magic show. The amorphous smoke provides no tangible place for him to grip. The bank's window of opportunity to wealth and power becomes a mirror whose multiple images dazzle and confuse.

In a world obscured by smoke and mirrors, Dean drifts easily into the character of Ballinger or, like Walter Mitty, into any number of other alluring roles. Even back in school he was easily diverted from the mundane to the exotic. When he had to write a report for biology on worms, he would look up the appropriate entry in the encyclopedia but then wander off to a more intriguing subject, like wombats. Later, as he spun rubber on the tire-builder machine at the factory, he "felt like the captain of a ship steering through a storm" (*LL*, 92). Now, when he cuts firewood, he becomes an athletic hero, and his noisy chainsaw "turns into the cheering section at a ball game" (92–93). In all of these cases, instead of molding his dreams into viable art, Dean becomes a victim of their whimsy. Robert Brinkmeyer observes that the arts of fiction and music can frequently liberate Mason's characters "from the confines of the solipsistic self."⁷⁸ In this story Dean's quasi art has just the opposite effect.

If Dean's fantasies for himself are expansive, his most lavish investment is in the dream that his daughter Jennifer can become a celebrated pianist. When Jennifer's piano teacher praises her progress and announces that she has long fingers well suited to play the piano, Dean promptly hitches his own dreams to this new artistic hope. Like an idol worshiper he takes Jennifer's hand and says admiringly, "I want to see them piano fingers" (*LL*, 93). One of the sound effects on Jennifer's new electronic keyboard is named cosmic tone. Dean cannot comprehend what this feature is, but he probably hopes that she can use it to approximate divine art by re-creating the music of the spheres. For him Jennifer's music suggests the power of alchemy. In contrast to his own base efforts, her performances earn gold stars, and he is certain that her first record will even go platinum.

Dean's highly leveraged dream displays a significant reversal of roles. Instead of the father supporting his young daughter, the child becomes a savior of the man. The most extensive use of Dean's own creative powers is to magnify the artistic ability of his daughter. Her talents will empower him, and he can revel vicariously in her success. In short, as the story's subtitle implies, his dreams quickly modulate into another key of being. Several details in the story suggest, however, that Jennifer's artistic success will not be forthcoming. The piano teacher who praises her may be senile, and Jennifer apparently plays no better than other students. Dean glorifies the electronic keyboard, but it actually "looks like trick false teeth flattened out into a big grin" (*LL*, 97). This clever metaphor suggests two degrees of removal from reality. Like Dean's fantasy scripts for a better television show, the keyboard is not just an imitation but rather a caricature of a copy. Furthermore, the big grin seems to mock Dean's inflated hopes. Caught up in fakery and illusion rather than the power of real art, Dean tries desperately to affirm Jennifer's unique talents. At the end of the story, he sees her as "someone he has suddenly dreamed into reality" (98). Unfortunately, just as his script for a television series is still a hollow dream, his grand hopes for Jennifer will no doubt remain equally insubstantial.

Despite his preoccupation with musical talent, Dean's dreams in the key of being never manage to achieve the proper pitch. Henri Bergson says that a comic effect results from "transposing the natural expression of an idea into another key."⁷⁹ Dean's imagined scripts for solving mysteries and his other Mittyesque fantasies are examples of such transpositions. Out of tune with reality, they become parodies of order rather than artistic means of creating it.

"A New-Wave Format" (1982)

In "A New-Wave Format" Mason displays the potential of popular art to transform and promote growth in those who are open to its powers. The story focuses on two very different kinds of music and two avid listeners. As an aspiring actress Sabrina is enthralled by the sentimental score of *Oklahoma!* Her middle-aged boyfriend, Edwin Creech, is an amateur disc jockey who gradually progresses to a profound appreciation of violent new-wave music.

Mason gives Edwin a mundane but revealing job—driving a bus that transports developmentally disabled adults to training classes. This job provides significant clues to Edwin's character and to a major theme of the story. At the age of 43, Edwin feels that his own development has been "a delayed reaction" (*S*, 222)—that he hasn't changed in the past 20 years—but within a few short weeks he experiences a dramatic spurt of personal growth. Ironically, he learns important lessons from his retarded passengers, and like them he acquires crucial "Living Skills" (218).

Edwin's previous work kept him detached from other people. In one typical job he worked on an offshore oil platform, and the remoteness of this setting paralleled his aloofness even from the other workers there. Back on land he drifted from job to job and from woman to woman. Since he never stayed in any situation long enough to develop real attachments, "he has gone through life rather blindly, without much pain or sense of loss" (*S*, 216). Edwin served briefly in the army, but there too he remained insulated. Because he never went to Vietnam with his contemporaries, "he feels that he has bypassed some critical stage in his life: a knowledge of terror" (217).

In his current job Edwin tries at first to maintain his distance and preserve superficial order, but the passengers clamor for his attention like overgrown children. Assuming instant intimacy, one insists on showing him the braces on her teeth every day, while another demands that he play songs from Elvis's Christmas album. For the first time Edwin has close contact with other humans and responsibility for their well-being. His extraordinary passengers arouse compassion that he has never before felt, and, filled with new confidence about routes and destinations, he thinks that he could drive them across the continent if necessary. Despite his job, however, Edwin's growth will derive not from travel but from art.

As Edwin finally grows up through immersion in disorder and chaos, the woman with whom he lives recedes further into callow youth. At the age of 20 Sabrina seems liberated and hip. She listens to the latest music, brushes with fennel toothpaste, and cooks unusual, arty dishes. At the moment, however, her ruling passion is the musical *Oklahoma!*, which Edwin considers "old-fashioned and phony" (*S*, 225). Sabrina has a minor role in an amateur production, but she talks pretentiously about "the 'artistic intention' of Rodgers and Hammerstein" (224). At night in the middle of the winter, she sings the summertime song "Oh, What a Beautiful Mornin' " and appears to believe all the Pollyannish promises of those lyrics. Sabrina is so caught up in her role that everything she does "seems like a performance" (221), and (as evidence of her larger disorientation) she confuses actors in the play (Jeff and Sue) with the roles they play (Curly and Laurey). In her enthusiasm for the theater, Sabrina is far from avant-garde. If *Oklahoma!* is old-fashioned, her next role—in *Life with Father*—will be a further reversion into an outmoded and sentimentalized past. In her playacting (and in living with a man old enough to be her father), Sabrina retains a childish outlook. As her stage, she elects a shallow world free of ugliness and pain. Thus, while Edwin progresses reluctantly into uncertain poststructuralist territory, Sabrina retreats to her cosily ordered quarters. Even if her anachronistic edifice is only a stage set, she cannot believe that this structure will ever fall down around her.

Because of their sharp differences in perspective, Sabrina and Edwin disagree vehemently about his passengers and especially about the art they produce. At one point Edwin shows Sabrina some stark black-and-white photographs taken by one of his passengers. These offbeat images of a sagging door, fried eggs on a cracked plate, and the rear end of a horse strike her as disgusting, and she can't bear to look. Edwin, however, is more receptive to the power of such art, and these same images reveal to him the vision of a true artist. Much like the stories of Lynnette in "Coyotes," such photographs show the artist's ability to "look at something and have a take on it. Not just take it for granted" (*LL*, 171). With appropriate concessions to political correctness, Mason uses a developmentally disabled character in much the same way that William Wordsworth presents a retarded child in his poem "The Idiot Boy." There the true visionary (and ultimate speaker in the poem) is "a person from whom intelligence has been stripped, so that there is between him and the natural world *nothing* but his capacity to discover in it its deep hidden secrets."[80]

In their stark intensity these examples of visual art from Edwin's passenger foreshadow the extreme music that will have an even more profound impact on Edwin. In both cases the works of art function through distortion—by moving beyond realism to some perspective that presents an exaggerated extreme of that realism. Linda Adams Barnes says that Mason's stories are "firmly rooted in the grotesque tradition of Flannery O'Connor."[81] O'Connor herself asserted that any literature that faithfully "mirrors society would be no fit guide for it."[82] On the other hand, literature that distorts by incorporating the grotesque becomes a trick mirror that inevitably captures a reader's attention and invites his interaction. The reader, as it were, postures before the trick mirror and asks if the reflection can really be his or her own. Embracing such a notion of the grotesque, Mason populates "A New-Wave Format" with characters who are developmentally disabled, she alludes to a photograph of a horse's posterior, and she incorporates bizarre music by groups like the Psychedelic Furs. Elements such as these intermingle the terrible with the comic. The grotesque music in particular jerks Edwin out of his insulated cocoon and instills that sense of pain and horror that he has evaded for 43 years.

While Sabrina's theatrical art narrows her perception of reality, Edwin's exposure to harsh popular music forces a more comprehensive vision. In the progression of musical selections Edwin plays for the passengers on his bus, Mason shows the stages of his personal development. At first he adopts a golden-oldies format, and the mellow songs of the 1960s have a calming, almost sedative effect. As Leslie White observes, such "safe programming" reflects Edwin's "counterfeit life of disengagement and prescription" (White, 74). Later, in reaction against "the sappy *Oklahoma!* sound track" (*S*, 221–22), his choices become more adventurous. He plays songs by the Jefferson Airplane, the Grateful Dead, and other "groups with vision" (222). Although he did not understand this music when he was younger, it "now seems full of possibility" (222). In deciding to play selections from the Doors, he opens his own portal to maturity. For him the Doors are a bridge spanning the "empty years" of his adult life and "connecting his youth solidly with the present" (228).

A few days before Christmas, a time of advent in Edwin's personal life as well as in the liturgical calendar, he shifts completely to a new-wave format, with cuts from the Plasmatics, Squeeze, and the Flying Lizards.

In this bold progression Edwin introduces music that is "violent and mindless" (*S*, 227). In fact, its frantic beat reminds him of "a crazed parent abusing a child, thrashing it senseless" (227). This new-wave music pumps his passengers up to a frenzy and eventually induces a seizure in a vulnerable young man named Ray. While the other passengers wail eerily, Edwin stops the bus, deals expertly with Ray's gagging and twitching, and switches to a carefree cassette by Donovan. Edwin receives praise for saving Ray's life, but he knows that the new-wave music probably created the problem. In playing such provocative music, however, Edwin has confronted the undeniable horrors of life just as he has faced the unpleasant but very real abnormalities of his passengers. The intensity of this violent music proves too much for his passengers, but it propels Edwin to greater maturity. What he missed in Vietnam, what was absent from his superficial life, courses through him now in this new wave. The music "sends Edwin inside for a look at the real source of his failures, and he comes to the uneasy realization that the meaning and worth of whatever one is comfortable with too often issue from the fear of its opposite" (White, 75).

Mason uses two nicely paired scenes to chart the course of Edwin's personal growth and to contrast it with Sabrina's immaturity. One scene occurs early in the story, the other on the final page. In both cases Edwin demonstrates to Sabrina his emergency medical techniques, but these demonstrations progress from the routine to the critical. In the early scene Edwin uses a fraternity paddle, a souvenir of Sabrina's year at college, to practice making a simple splint for a broken leg. Thus, he takes something essentially frivolous and transforms it into an orthopedic device. Sabrina grudgingly allows him to practice on her body but is appalled at the mere thought of breaking her leg. She fears both the physical pain and the disappointment of not being able to act in *Oklahoma!* Stuck in adolescent blindness, she does not yet understand that suffering can bring strength and loss can lead to fulfillment.

In the story's final scene Edwin declares that he is no longer "practicing" emergency techniques because he is "beyond that" (*S*, 231). After four decades of slowly preparing for life, he is at last really experiencing it. Now he has moved past splints to cardiopulmonary resuscitation. Instead of working on Sabrina's extremities, he focuses on the central organ of life, her heart. In asking her to pretend that she has a terrible pain right in the middle of her chest, he tries to educate her not just about cardiac disease but about the power of empathy. By treating her deficiency in feeling, he hopes to guide her through the same lessons he has mastered by playing such disturbing music on his bus. There he provided emergency resuscitation for Ray. At the same time Edwin himself experienced a symbolic rebirth. Now, by educating Sabrina's heart and making her open to the transforming power of pain, he tries to lead her also to a fuller life. Instead of merely performing in an old-fashioned play with the word "life" in its title, she can perhaps begin to live it directly.

In distinguishing Mason's use of the grotesque from that of O'Connor, Linda Adams Barnes observes that stories by Mason lack the "consolation of O'Connor's Christian faith" (Barnes, 133). Indeed, the inhabitants of Mason's postmodern ruburbs cannot readily discover either consolation or faith. Nevertheless, the experience of Edwin confirms that the most unlikely art can sometimes inspire vision, just as, in a story like O'Connor's "Good Country People," bizarre characters and improbable events compel insight. "A New-Wave Format" and other Mason stories are surely "not devoid of characters experiencing O'Connoresque redemption" (Barnes, 140).

"Love Life" (1984)

The title story of Mason's second collection focuses on the love lives of women representing two very different generations. Neither woman is a producing artist, but both are fervent art appreciators. The representative of the older generation is Opal Freeman, a retired schoolteacher who has lived in the small town of Hopewell all her life, had limited experiences with men, and remained unmarried. Opal's niece Jenny is "enough like Opal to be her own daughter" (*LL*, 2), but she displays the attitudes and styles of a new era. Jenny's wandering life has taken her from coast to coast, and her relationships with men have been so numerous that Opal can't keep track of all the names she has mentioned.

To develop this counterpoint of different generations, Mason introduces two distinctive groups of images from radically different art forms. One consists of artifacts from the dying past—intricate patchwork quilts handed down to Opal by her ancestors. In stark contrast, the second group of images is a product of the electronic age—a cultural icon of the volatile present. These surreal and constantly changing images come from music videos broadcast on MTV.

Having established two generations of women and two striking groups of artistic images, Mason executes a surprising crossover (one even more dramatic than that of the two generations in "A New-Wave

Format"). Here Opal gleefully shatters the stereotype of spinster schoolteacher by sitting for hours in front of her television set. With volume pumped up to the maximum, she hungrily watches the rapidly morphing MTV images and seeks insight from this seemingly chaotic postmodern art. Opal has lived with the old ways and long resented their limitations. Now, as the surname Freeman implies, she embraces the freedom of a new age. Jenny, in sharp contrast, repeatedly begs her aunt Opal to bring out the old quilts. She has experienced sexual liberation and freedom of the road but now yearns for the firm anchors of heritage and the stability of home. Such a chiasmatic pattern invites us to reexamine the values and experiences of both characters. The persistent glow from a television set may illuminate dark corners of Opal's life. Against the complex background of a patchwork quilt, Jenny's character may emerge in sharper focus.

Obviously Opal's memories of her small-town past offer little comfort as she ages. Before retirement Opal taught mathematics at Hopewell High, but the precision of that discipline provided no reassurance or aesthetic satisfaction. Instead of Euclidean beauty and order, she recalls only mathematical enigmas. Her dreams are still filled with "complicated quadratic equations with shifting values and no solutions" (*LL*, 2)—algebraic equivalents of her perplexing life.

Opal has been intimate with more than one man, but those experiences from the past are sharply severed from her present. Brief and pursued in secrecy (out of fear of losing her job), Opal's sexual encounters were escapes into another world—adventures in a parallel but remote universe. She recalls one night in a Nashville motel room that was totally "devoid of history and association" (*LL*, 11). Such a setting neatly isolated immediate actions from prior experience. To further insure that the present would not impinge on the future, Opal tidied up the room "to make it as neat as if she had never been there" (11).

Without a store of memories to sustain her, Opal feeds from the cornucopia of music video images. In these inventive and sexually suggestive scenes, she discovers a bold repudiation of the provincial values that limited her own behavior. Fear of community disapproval made her life rigid, compartmentalized, and unfulfilled, but characters in the videos "change and flow with the music" (*LL*, 1). In one video, for example, a dangerous woman eludes numerous policemen by running through an icy meat locker, jumping a roadblock on a motorcycle, and slipping onto a train. As she glides so easily away from the authorities, she waves a smiling goodbye. Outwardly a respectable spinster but really a rebel at heart, Opal too can take vicarious delight in this triumph of id over superego.

Music videos celebrate freedom both in their fluid artistic form and in their content, but their appeal to Opal is more complex. In one of her favorite videos, a teenaged boy grows cat whiskers and long claws, ghouls escape from their coffins, and Vincent Price makes scary noises in the background. Such bizarre details (apparently from the video for Michael Jackson's "Thriller") speak eloquently to Opal about the terrors of growing up and growing old. For Opal the video dramatizes the fears hidden inside all young people as they experience the dramatic changes of adolescence and face an uncertain future as adults. Ultimately in each individual life "an old person waits, a nearly dead body that can still dance" (*LL*, 11). As intimations of this inescapable fate, the video ghouls are frightening, but even in the grip of death they continue to celebrate life by dancing. After watching the scary video, Opal feels strangely relaxed and comforted. Her arthritic joints are now loose, and she is ready to continue the inevitable dance toward death. Opal's recurring dreams about mathematical equations show her impulse to create order, but such dreams lead only to enigmas. In the dreamlike video art, however, she finds liberating catharsis.

As testimony to the artistic power of MTV, Sue Lorch describes music videos as the contemporary equivalents of seventeenth-century metaphysical poetry. The music videos devoured by Opal usually display temporal and spatial disjunctions, conjunctions without apparent connections, synesthetic interplay, and bold self-reflexiveness. According to Lorch, these stylistic features function in music video art much as paradox and metaphysical conceit did in the poetry of John Donne. Such unpredictable features startle the audience and urge it on to new awareness.[83]

Both Opal and Jenny have embarked on significant passages in life, but they have charted divergent courses. The aging woman travels an electronic road away from Hopewell while the young adult, a recursive traveler like Mary in "Residents and Transients," valiantly attempts to go home again. After her return to Hopewell, Jenny is obsessed by scenes of incompleteness. During her first two days back home, she sees "two people with artificial legs, a blind man, a man with hooks for hands, and a man without an arm" (*LL*, 3). Later, when she goes with friends to a bar in Hopkinsville, she is acutely aware that the singer has a prosthetic limb hidden under her jeans and that her accompanist is blind. Sights such as these may not be so unusual, but the degree to which they dominate Jenny's perception is telling. By focusing so persistently on external evidences of fragmentation, she projects her own inner deficiencies.

Since Jenny's life is incomplete and her links to home are weak, she tries to solve her problems by purchasing land. Even though she clearly needs a more dependable car, the emblem of her former role as traveler, she hunts instead for a place where she can grow tomatoes. Apparently she has had enough of random movement and wants to court the pastoral by putting down roots along with her tomato seedlings. At one point her pastoral feelings for the land and her aesthetic attraction to old quilts converge. After buying a small plot, she describes it as her "block on the quilt" (*LL*, 13). Since quilt blocks make pieces of a puzzle fit together neatly, this art form has special appeal to Jenny.

Despite Jenny's reverent attempts to find order in old quilts, those in Opal's closet present ambiguous texts that may invite divergent readings. Like the quilts in Joyce Carol Oates's "Celestial Timepiece," they display a "Babel of textures."[84] Some of the traditional patterns in Opal's collection clearly imply positive values. For example, the double wedding ring quilt with its careful repetitions of interconnected circles is a graphic celebration of constancy and fidelity. Similarly, the star quilts with their sharp points may suggest clarity of direction and navigational certainty. On the other hand, the "haphazard shapes" of the crazy quilts conjure up, even for Jenny, images of "odd, twisted lives" (*LL*, 10). Opal reads the entire collection of quilts in a decidedly negative way. For her they tell the stories of "miserable, cranky women, straining their eyes, stitching on those dark scraps of material" (15). Instead of reaffirming traditional values, the quilts testify to past oppression of women. Opal quilted some in the past, but she has now abandoned her needle and grasped her television remote-control paddle.

One specific quilt illustrates the sharp divergence between Opal and Jenny. This "burial quilt" has dark blocks of wool on which off-white tombstones have been appliquéd. On the tombstones are names, birth dates, and dates of death for members of the Freeman family. The quilt is irregular in shape with an open edge so more blocks can be added as family members die. Opal considers the quilt "too ugly to put on a bed and too morbid to work on" (*LL*, 15), but to Jenny it is gorgeous. For Opal the quilt is a plague and a burden, but for Jenny it provides inspiration to study the family tree and to become an artist herself by learning to quilt.

In her admiration of all the old quilts, Jenny's socioaesthetic values coincide with changing feminist attitudes toward needlework. For generations the act of sewing confined women simply because their families required clothing and bedding. By the late nineteenth century, when the rise of industrial production liberated many women from the necessity of sewing, fancier needlework emerged as a mode of confinement that could be even more oppressive. Then, with a pronounced emphasis on quality rather than quantity, "the model wife or daughter was one who sewed, quilted, embroidered, knitted, crocheted, and tatted items worthy of admiration." Not by coincidence, such a woman also "sat quietly, modestly, and patiently and selflessly engaged in the repetition, monotony, and routine of the women's sphere."[85] Any woman who tried to enlarge or escape this sphere might very well be told, as was the poet Anne Bradstreet, that her hand was better suited for a needle than a pen.

In its earliest stages, then, the modern feminist movement pointed out how needlework had restricted women's choices, and it typically regarded quilting as just another emblem of women's inequality. As feminist discourse matured and the status of quilts rose in the art world (especially after the 1971 exhibition at the Whitney Museum, "Abstract Design in American Quilts"), their value among feminists also escalated. Since quilts were "no longer a necessity" and were "no longer used to enforce standards of femininity," they could "now become a banner of feminism" (Behuniak-Long, 156). As a member of a younger generation, Jenny can unfurl this new banner. Still a victim of the more restrictive past, Opal is unable to embrace such a reinterpretation of quilts.

Even if Jenny agrees with current feminist values, her passion for quilts indicates not so much a political agenda as a deep personal need to establish connections. Many aspects of quilts and the quilting process make this an especially rich metaphor for exploring Jenny's aspirations. Susan Behuniak-Long asserts that "the act of quilting is the act of connection" since "pieces are stitched together, blocks joined, borders attached, and layers quilted and bound." In a more expansive sense, quilting joins women of different historical times or different places who have all shared in this form of expression. Finally, "teaching the craft of quilting binds generations, friends, communities" (Behuniak-Long, 166). Such binding together has eluded Jenny on her travels, and she seeks it now in an old and homely craft.

Jenny's resolutions to explore history and traditional handicrafts may be worthwhile, but the burial quilt also unleashes an unwelcome part of her past—a torrent of unresolved grief. As powerful a work of art as a music video, this quilt makes Jenny recall the accidental death of Jim, a boyfriend with whom she traveled throughout the West. Actually, Jenny had broken up with Jim long before his death because Jim was himself preoccupied with grief. Jim felt guilty because his brother had died in Vietnam. In response to this multidimensional grief that interrupted the flow of two lives, Opal's advice is simply, "Don't look back, hon" (*LL*, 17). In support of such homely wisdom, Opal can cite her favorite music videos as paradigms. With their constantly morphing images, they are emphatic object lessons in adaptation. They dramatize chaotic change but also display graceful, flowing responses to that change. Reminiscent of the time-lapse photographs in "Nancy Culpepper," the music video images are even more pronounced in their artistic strategy.

Mason's story ends just as it began—focusing on Opal rather than Jenny, on the art of music videos rather than that of quilts. In the dialogue between generations, the wisdom of age triumphs gently over the callowness of youth. But in the debate between cultural icons, the energy of the strikingly new art form displaces the apparent morbidity of the old. As the story ends, Opal watches a video that shows a woman "lying on her stomach on a car hood in a desert full of gas pumps" (*LL*, 17). No doubt Opal is much older than this woman, but she too still has plenty of fuel to keep herself moving. Later in the video a teacher "with her white hair in a bun" looks disapprovingly at her unruly students but is actually "thinking about how, when the bell rings, she will hit the road to Nashville" (18). This teacher on the television screen is a projection of Opal's irrepressible vitality. Even though her own trips to Nashville were not always satisfactory, she continues to celebrate life and absorb the power of the MTV art pulsating all around her. Robert Brinkmeyer's excessively harsh reading of this story finds "no sense of restorative order." Instead, he sees Opal "locked in an eternal present of disordered images, making no efforts . . . to discover with song" (Brinkmeyer, 1988–89, 16). To be sure, the art that surrounds Opal is confusing, but the end product is not confusion. From this vibrant electronic art, Opal derives both energy and new insight.

In light of Opal's spirited response to music videos, perhaps we should read the story's title not as a noun phrase but as a command. As a mere phrase the title would presumably refer to romantic episodes that were themselves truncated and disconnected from the rest of Opal's life. As a complete sentence in the imperative mood, the title invokes an attitude that can make life expansive and full.

Conclusion

Mason's travelers are not great explorers; her gardeners will not grow prize-winning produce; her aspiring artists are not likely to receive loud acclaim. Indeed, all of the stories discussed here provide evidence of Mason's deliberate attention to "the lives of so-called ordinary people, people whose lives weren't written about much before." Mason's stories ignore the grand quests of romantic heroes, the eloquent ruminations of aesthetes, and focus instead on the average "person's struggle to get by in a mass society." In electing these limitations, however, Mason does not crawl headfirst into the cramped quarters of extreme minimalism. She asserts that the difficulties and dreams of ordinary people "are nevertheless complicated and rich."[86] Her limited domain still offers abundant space for intriguing characters, engaging struggles, perplexing questions about conduct and values.

Although Mason has been criticized for her frequent use of open endings, such conclusions are an important means of maintaining her chosen artistic and philosophical position.[87] If the assumptions of postmodern fiction do not compel open endings, Mason's own premises frequently invite them. She displays characters searching for order on the road and in the garden, or trying to create order through their art or craft. At best such order is elusive, but if any character can plausibly achieve some degree of success, Mason displays the favorable conclusion. More often, however, when the effort is stalemated or inconclusive, Mason declines to provide a neat ending.

According to Joseph Flora, open endings give "the sense that the characters, not the narrator, will play the next scene."[88] By avoiding artificially neat resolutions, Mason leaves her characters free to act. As the stories conclude, some characters, like Mack in "The Rookers" or Steve in "Midnight Magic," remain hopelessly bewildered. Many others, however, have progressed through turmoil and confusion to greater insight. Like Norma Jean on the bank of the Tennessee River in "Shiloh" or Liz with her toe in a hot tub in "Sorghum," a number of Mason's protagonists are poised to take decisive action—to mount a new assault on the ambient disorder. In the uncharted fictional future they face numerous problems but also enjoy many possibilities.

The boundaries of Mason's fictional domain are tightly drawn, but it is hardly the moral wasteland found in some minimalist fiction. Indeed, her fertile ground sprouts numerous questions about values even if it fails to bring the desired answers to ripeness. Mason's stories examine important social issues like abortion, divorce, and care of the elderly, but they never become polemical. Her work is seriously concerned with moral questions but is never moralistic. When her characters behave foolishly, like Steve in "Midnight Magic," she avoids stooping to parody. When they suffer personal tragedies, like Ruth in "Bumblebees," she carefully skirts sentimentality. The trick, she says, is getting "just the right distance from the characters—not too close, not too far—so that they can be taken seriously."[89] As a narrator she wants to avoid the implicit moralism of either excessive criticism or overindulgence. Thus, the moral force of a story derives from a character's own actions.

Linda Adams Barnes suggests that Mason "offers her generation the only kind of morality that it will accept by merely dramatizing the incongruities resulting from the clash between traditional Southern life and encroaching modern life." Such dramatizations become instructive simply because they display her characters as survivors. Even though they must "compromise, adjust, and conform," they manage to cope. Thus, "Mason's ultimate message is 'Do the best you can'" (Bames, 139).

Notes to Part 1

1. Judith Freeman, "Country Parables" [a review of *Love Life*], *Los Angeles Times Book Review*, 19 March 1989, 1.

2. Bobbie Ann Mason, *Shiloh and Other Stories* (New York: Harper & Row, 1982), 115; hereafter cited in the text as *S*.

3. Bobbie Ann Mason, "Reaching the Stars: My Life as a Fifties Groupie," in *A World Unsuspected: Portraits of Southern Childhood*, ed. Alex Harris (Chapel Hill: University of North Carolina Press, 1987), 55.

4. Lila Havens, "Residents and Transients: An Interview with Bobbie Ann Mason," *Crazyhorse* 29 (Fall 1985): 95; hereafter cited in the text as Havens.

5. Quoted in Albert E. Wilhelm, "Private Rituals: Coping with Change in the Fiction of Bobbie Ann Mason," *Midwest Quarterly* 28 (Winter 1987): 272; hereafter cited in the text as Wilhelm 1987.

6. Darlene Reimers Hill, " 'Use to the Menfolks Would Eat First': Food and Food Rituals in the Fiction of Bobbie Ann Mason," *Southern Quarterly* 30 (Winter–Spring 1992): 83; hereafter cited in the text as Darlene Hill.

7. Maureen Ryan, "Stopping Places: Bobbie Ann Mason's Short Stories," in *Women Writers of the Contemporary South*, ed. Peggy Whitman Prenshaw (Jackson: University Press of Mississippi, 1984), 294.

8. R. Z. Sheppard, "Neighbors" [a review of *Shiloh and Other Stories*], *Time*, 3 January 1983, 88.

9. Mark A. R. Facknitz, "Raymond Carver and the Menace of Minimalism," *CEA Critic* 52 (Fall 1989–Winter 1990): 62; hereafter cited in the text as Facknitz.

10. Michael Gorra, "Laughter and Bloodshed," *Hudson Review* 37 (Spring 1980): 155.

11. John Barth, "A Few Words about Minimalism," *Weber Studies* 4 (1987): 8; hereafter cited in the text as Barth.

12. James Atlas,"Less Is Less," *Atlantic*, June 1981, 97.

13. Madison Bell, "Less Is Less: The Dwindling American Short Story," *Harper's*, April 1986, 65.

14. Enid Shomer, "An Interview with Bobbie Ann Mason," *Black Warrior Review* 12 (Spring 1986): 96; hereafter cited in the text as Shomer.

15. Dorothy Combs Hill, "An Interview with Bobbie Ann Mason," *Southern Quarterly* 31 (Fall 1992): 105; hereafter cited in the text as Dorothy Hill.

16. Wendy Smith, "*PW* Interviews Bobbie Ann Mason," *Publishers Weekly*, 30 August 1985, 425; hereafter cited in the text as Wendy Smith.

17. Richard Giannone, "Bobbie Ann Mason and the Recovery of Mystery," *Studies in Short Fiction* 27 (Fall 1990): 554–55.

18. Bobbie Ann Mason, *The Girl Sleuth* (Athens: University of Georgia Press, 1995), x; hereafter cited in the text as *Sleuth*.

19. Bobbie Ann Mason, "The Way We Lived: The Chicken Tower," *New Yorker*, 18 October 1995, 90; hereafter cited in the text as "Way."

20. Greg Johnson, "Stories of the New South," *Southwest Review* 68 (Spring 1983): 196–97.

21. Lewis A. Lawson, "The Grotesque in Recent Southern Fiction," in *Patterns of Commitment in American Literature*, ed. Marston LaFrance (Toronto: University of Toronto Press, 1967), 177.

22. James Reason, *Man in Motion: The Psychology of Travel* (New York: Walker Press, 1974), 2–3.

23. Jean Corwin, "Identity in the Victorian Travel Narrative" (Ph.D. diss., Indiana University, 1987), 5.

24. Bobbie Ann Mason, *Love Life* (New York: Harper & Row, 1989), 21; hereafter cited in the text as *LL*.

25. Bonnie Lyons and Bill Oliver, "An Interview with Bobbie Ann Mason," *Contemporary Literature* 32 (1991): 464.

26. Marshall Blonsky, *American Mythologies* (New York: Oxford University Press, 1992), 13; hereafter cited in the text as Blonsky.

27. Michal Smith, "Bobbie Ann Mason, Artist and Rebel," *Kentucky Review* 8 (Autumn 1988): 57.

28. Arthur Asa Berger, *Signs in Contemporary Culture: An Introduction to Semiotics* (New York: Longman, 1984), 170–72.

29. Octavio Paz, "Eroticism and Gastrosophy," *Daedalus* 101 (Fall 1972): 75.

30. Bobbie Ann Mason, *Spence + Lila (New York: Harper & Row, 1988), 57.*

31. Anatole Broyard, [a review of *Shiloh and Other Stories*], *New York Times*, 23 November 1982, C14.

32. Orrin E. Klapp, *Inflation of Symbols: Loss of Value in American Culture* (New Brunswick, N.J.: Transaction, 1991), 3.

33. Charles Newman, *The Post-Modern Aura: The Act of Fiction in an Age of Inflation* (Evanston, Ill.: Northwestern University Press, 1985), 6.

34. Craig Gholson, "Bobbie Ann Mason," *BOMB* 28 (Summer 1989): 42; hereafter cited in the text as Gholson.

35. George H. Lewis, "Community through Exclusion and Illusion: The Creation of Social Worlds in an American Shopping Mall," *Journal of Popular Culture* 24 (Fall 1990): 123.

36. Robert Fulton, "Death, Grief and the Funeral in Contemporary Society," in *The Dying Human*, ed. Andre de Vries and Amnon Carmi (Ramat Gan, Israel: Turtledove, 1979), 461.

37. Jane Littlewood, "The Denial of Death and Rites of Passage in Contemporary Societies," in *The Sociology of Death*, ed. David Clark (Oxford: Blackwell, 1993), 76; hereafter cited in the text as Littlewood.

38. Leslie White, "The Function of Popular Culture in Bobbie Ann Mason's *Shiloh and Other Stories* and *In Country*," *Southern Quarterly* 26 (Summer 1988): 70–73; hereafter cited in the text as White.

39. Raymond Firth, *Symbols: Public and Private* (Ithaca, N.Y.: Cornell University Press, 1973), 376.

40. Margaret Visser, *The Rituals of Dinner: The Origins, Evolution, Eccentricities, and Meaning of Table Manners* (New York: Grove Weidenfeld, 1991), 27; hereafter cited in the text as Visser.

41. Karen Underwood, "Mason's 'Drawing Names,' " *Explicator* 48 (Spring 1990): 231–32.

42. Carolyn G. Heilbrun, "What Was Penelope Unweaving," in *Hamlet's Mother and Other Women* (New York: Columbia University Press, 1990), 108.

43. Albert E. Wilhelm, "An Interview with Bobbie Ann Mason," *Southern Quarterly* 26 (Winter 1988): 35–36; hereafter cited in the text as Wilhelm, 1988.

44. Mordecai Marcus, "What Is an Initiation Story?" *Journal of Aesthetics and Art Criticism* 19 (Winter 1960): 223.

45. Leslie A. Fiedler, *No! in Thunder* (Boston: Beacon Press, 1960), 279.

46. Bobbie Ann Mason, "Recreation," *Bloodroot* (Winter 1981): 11–23.

47. Susan Sontag, *On Photography* (New York: Farrar, Straus and Giroux, 1977), 163; hereafter cited in the text as Sontag.

48. G. O. Morphew, "Downhome Feminists in *Shiloh and Other Stories,*" *Southern Literary Journal* 21 (Spring 1989): 48.

49. Orrin E. Klapp, *Collective Search for Identity* (New York: Holt, Rinehart, and Winston, 1969), 28.

50. Raymond Carver, comment from dustjacket of *Shiloh and Other Stories.*

51. Bobbie Ann Mason, *Nabokov's Garden: A Guide to* Ada (Ann Arbor, Mich.: Ardis, 1974), 15; hereafter cited in the text as *Garden.*

52. Leo Marx, *The Machine in the Garden: Technology and the Pastoral Ideal in America* (New York: Oxford University Press, 1964), 25.

53. Bobbie Ann Mason, "Creating Meaning out of the Chaos," *Baltimore Evening Sun,* 12 April 1988, A19; hereafter cited in the text as "Creating."

54. Tina Bucher, "Changing Roles and Finding Stability: Women in Bobbie Ann Mason's *Shiloh and Other Stories,*" *Border States: Journal of the Kentucky-Tennessee American Studies Association* 8 (1991): 54.

55. Robin Becker, "Fear-of-Success Stories?" *Women's Review of Books* 1 (April 1984): 5–6.

56. Bobbie Ann Mason, "Hear My Song," *New Yorker,* 20 March 1995, 110.

57. Annette Kolodny, *The Lay of the Land: Metaphor as Experience and History in American Life and Letters* (Chapel Hill: University of North Carolina Press, 1975), 3–9.

58. Elizabeth Jane Harrison, *Female Pastoral: Women Writers Re-Visioning the American South* (Knoxville: University of Tennessee Press, 1991), 133–34.

59. Lucinda MacKethan, *The Dream of Arcady: Place and Time in Southern Literature* (Baton Rouge: Louisiana State University Press, 1980), 215.

60. Nina Auerbach; *Communities of Women: An Idea in Fiction* (Cambridge, Mass.: Harvard University Press, 1978), 3.

61. Barbara T. Ryan, "Decentered Authority in Bobbie Ann Mason's *In Country,*" *Critique* 31 (Spring 1990): 211.

62. Arnold van Gennep, *The Rites of Passage,* trans. Monika B. Vizedom and Gabrielle L. Caffee (Chicago: University of Chicago Press, 1960), 4.

63. Barbara Henning, "Minimalism and the American Dream: 'Shiloh' by Bobbie Ann Mason and 'Preservation' by Raymond Carver," *Modern Fiction Studies* 35 (Winter 1989): 694.

64. Adrienne Rich, *Of Woman Born: Motherhood as Experience and Institution* (New York: Norton, 1976), 225; hereafter cited in the text as Rich.

65. Marianne Hirsch, *The Mother/Daughter Plot: Narrative, Psychoanalysis, Feminism* (Bloomington: Indiana University Press, 1989), 133.

66. Fredric Jameson, "Postmodernism and Consumer Society," in *The Anti-Aesthetic: Essays on Postmodern Culture,* ed. Hal Foster (Seattle, Wash.: Bay Press, 1983), 125.

67. Robert H. Brinkmeyer Jr., "Finding One's History: Bobbie Ann Mason

and Contemporary Southern Literature," *Southern Literary Journal* 19 (Spring 1987): 22; hereafter cited in the text as Brinkmeyer, 1987.

68. Thomas R. Cole, *The Journey of Life: A Cultural History of Aging in America* (Cambridge: Cambridge University Press, 1992), 242.

69. Margaret Morganroth Gullette, *Safe at Last in the Middle Years* (Berkeley: University of California Press, 1988), 41–46.

70. Mircea Eliade, *Birth and Rebirth* (New York: Harper, 1958), xii.

71. Michael Marsden, "Television Viewing as Ritual," in *Rituals and Ceremonies in Popular Culture*, ed. Ray B. Browne (Bowling Green, Ohio: Bowling Green University Popular Press, 1980), 121.

72. Jeff Ferrell, "Degradation and Rehabilitation in Popular Culture," *Journal of Popular Culture* 24 (Winter 1990): 90–92.

73. Harold Bloom, *The Anxiety of Influence* (New York: Oxford University Press, 1973), 5.

74. Robert B. Ray, "Postmodernism," in *Encyclopedia of Literature and Criticism*, ed. Martin Coyle et al (Detroit: Gale Research, 1991), 135; hereafter cited in the text as Ray.

75. Edward Ball, "The Great Sideshow of the Situationist International," *Yale French Studies* 73 (1987): 34.

76. Dennis Vannatta, "Theme and Structure in Tim O'Brien's *Going After Cacciato*," *Modern Fiction Studies* 28 (1982): 244.

77. Jerome Klinkowitz, *Structuring the Void: The Struggle for Subject in Contemporary American Fiction* (Durham, N.C.: Duke University Press, 1992), 155; hereafter cited in the text as Klinkowitz.

78. Robert H. Brinkmeyer Jr., "Never Stop Rocking: Bobbie Ann Mason and Rock and Roll," *Mississippi Quarterly* 42 (Winter 1988–89): 9; hereafter cited in the text as Brinkmeyer, 1988–89.

79. Quoted in Wylie Sypher, *Comedy* (Garden City, N.Y.: Doubleday Anchor, 1956), 140.

80. David Ferry, *The Limits of Mortality* (Middletown, Conn.: Wesleyan University Press, 1959), 98.

81. Linda Adams Barnes, "The Freak Endures: The Southern Grotesque from Flannery O'Connor to Bobbie Ann Mason," in *Since Flannery O'Connor: Essays on the Contemporary Short Story*, ed. Loren Logsden and Charles W. Mayer (Macomb: Western Illinois University Press, 1987), 140; hereafter cited in the text as Barnes.

82. Flannery O'Connor, *Mystery and Manners*, ed. Sally and Robert Fitzgerald (New York: Farrar, Straus & Giroux, 1961), 46.

83. Sue Lorch, "Metaphor, Metaphysics, and MTV," *Journal of Popular Culture* 22 (Winter 1988): 152.

84. Joyce Carol Oates, *Celestial Timepiece: Poems* (Dallas, Tex.: Pressworks, 1980), 24–25.

85. Susan Behuniak-Long, "Preserving the Social Fabric: Quilting in a

Technological World," in *Quilt Culture: Tracing the Pattern,* ed. Cheryl B. Torsney and Judy Elsley (Columbia: University of Missouri Press, 1994), 153–54; hereafter cited in the text as Behuniak-Long.

86. Bobbie Ann Mason, [untitled contribution to "A Symposium on Contemporary American Fiction"], in *Writers and Their Craft: Short Stories & Essays on the Narrative,* ed. Nicholas Delbanco and Laurence Goldstein (Detroit, Mich.: Wayne State University Press, 1991), 176–77.

87. Robert Towers, "American Graffiti" [a review of *Shiloh and Other Stories*], *New York Review of Books,* 16 December 1982, 40.

88. Joseph M. Flora, "Bobbie Ann Mason," in *Contemporary Fiction Writers of the South,* ed. Joseph M. Flora and Robert Bain (Westport, Conn.: Greenwood Press, 1993), 277.

89. Bobbie Ann Mason, [untitled introduction to "Shiloh"], in *American Voices: Best Short Fiction by Contemporary Authors,* ed. Sally Arteseros (New York: Hyperion, 1992), 335.

Part 2

THE WRITER

Introduction

Even though Mason earned graduate degrees in literature and published a scholarly commentary on Nabokov's *Ada*, she has not written extensively about her own works. She has provided (in *American Voices*) a short introduction to her best-known story, "Shiloh," and in 1991 she contributed a brief essay to a book entitled *Writers and Their Craft*. Another essay entitled "Creating Meaning out of the Chaos" charts the evolution of Mason's first published story and contains some of her most direct comments about the process of writing fiction. Written while Mason was a Jane and Robert Meyerhoff Visiting Professor at Goucher College, this essay appeared in the *Baltimore Evening Sun*.

Several interviews with Mason are available in popular magazines, trade publications (like *Publishers Weekly*), and scholarly journals. In excerpts reprinted here from a 1991 interview with Bonnie Lyons and Bill Oliver, Mason contrasts her own protagonists with earlier literary heroes. She also comments on minimalist fiction (a label frequently applied to her stories), discusses her experiments with point of view, and points out some differences between stories in *Shiloh* and those in *Love Life*.

The second selection in this section is the text of an interview provided by Mason especially for this volume. This interview took place in October 1995 after Mason's appearance at the Southern Festival of Books in Nashville, Tennessee. In this interview she discusses, among other things, her fondness for jigsaw puzzles, the impact of graduate study on her writing, her affinity with Nabokov, and the importance of place (specifically, western Kentucky) in her stories.

An Interview with Bobbie Ann Mason

Bonnie Lyons and Bill Oliver

We met Bobbie Ann Mason in her hometown of Mayfield, Kentucky (population 12,000), where many of her stories are set. Before the interview, she drove us around the town, showing us the cemetery with its silver-painted iron gate donated by the Daughters of the Confederacy, the grain company whose elevator is said to be the tallest structure in western Kentucky, the town square with its Victorian courthouse and new jail annex, and the ramshackle white house used as Emmett's and Sam's home in the film version of Mason's first novel, *In Country*.

Mason talked about the film as she drove, said she liked it very much and also liked the people she met who worked on it. She didn't get to see the actual filming, because there was a rule barring the author's presence—a standard Hollywood practice, since writers sometimes prove meddlesome. ("They needn't have worried about me," Mason said.)

Her younger sister, LaNelle, who did the illustrations for Mason's most recent novel, *Spence + Lila*, had her life altered by the filming. A former art student with a degree from the University of Kentucky, she was working at the local Photomat when she began dating the film's art director. Later they married and she moved to California. Now LaNelle is with her husband in Australia, where he builds theme parks for MGM. Mason recounts this story of sudden and dramatic change—the kind that seldom occurs in her own writing—with obvious relish and faint disbelief.

We go by the family farm, where Mason's mother still lives. (Her father died last year.) The small, brown farmhouse sits close to the highway. Behind it, the fields—"Spence's fields"—fall away to a tree-lined creek two hundred yards distant. There's a white picnic table behind the house; a dog (Oscar) and a cat (Abraham), both of whom appear in *Spence + Lila*, are asleep on the table. The farm now lies within expanded city limits, but as a child Mason attended a country school,

From *Contemporary Literature* 32 (1991): 449–70. © 1991 by the University of Wisconsin Press. Reprinted by permission.

with "terrible teachers and poor students." She longed then, she says, to go to school in Mayfield, to be a "city" child.

We have our interview in the restaurant of the Mayfield Holiday Inn, where Mason's nephew is the night clerk. She has little to say about her work in progress, a historical novel set in western Kentucky at the turn of the century. "Actually, I'm really eager to get back to short stories." Not that the novel isn't going well: "It's just bad luck to talk about it, because then you might not do it." She has a good deal to say about her other work, however, including *Love Life* (1989), *Spence + Lila* (1988), *In Country* (1985), and *Shiloh and Other Stories* (1982).

Q. In an earlier interview, when asked about your taking up fiction writing fairly late in life, you started out by saying that your experience set up a number of roadblocks to the imagination but ended by wondering whether, in an environment that totally encouraged creativity, "there would be any incentive whatsoever to resist, to bust out, any build-up of energy." Do you think there is an ideal balance between repression and encouragement? Did you need to encounter a certain amount of resistance?

A. I've often wondered what I would have done with my life if I had gotten a lot of advantages from the very beginning. I did start writing when I was eleven, but along the way I was stymied quite a lot. I don't know if it's necessary for everybody to have something to resist against for creative energy to build up. It just seems to be the way it happens at times. I think about Nabokov who, to hear him describe it, had an ideal childhood. He had every advantage. He was pampered and indulged. I wonder what it would have been like for him if he hadn't been exiled and if his father hadn't been assassinated. We know that those experiences are the formation of his fiction and that's what his sensibility acts upon. I wonder if he had stayed in that comfortable place where he was the most important person in the world, if he would have anything interesting to tell us. I don't know.

Q. I sense that you have a rebellious strain, that some part of you is impelled to act against whatever people say you ought to be doing or ought to be writing.

A. You've hit it, haven't you? Because I was going to be that way about half of your questions. Actually I was going to try not to be that way because the last interview I did turned out to be perverse and not

111

as polite as it should have been. I don't know, it is a very quiet rebellion. I'm not outspoken or politically verbal. I don't get upset very easily. I'm a stoic person. I don't get angry. I sit quietly in the corner and say "no."

Q. Isn't your writing a way of saying "no" in certain respects?

A. I'm glad you see that.

Q. You write about people, places, and subjects that others might tend to dismiss as not very "literary." Do you see yourself as reclaiming materials that otherwise would be lost or ignored?

A. Yes, it's somewhat natural for me to feel that way. I have my material, what's been allotted to me. And along with that comes a Southern defensive posture and a desire to reclaim a measure of pride and identity for my people.

Q. There's a passage in *In Country* in which a dilapidated barn is described. It's said to be like an artifact from dinosaur times. Are you something of an archaeologist trying to recapture pieces of the past?

A. There are ways of doing that. I don't like to think of myself as romanticizing the quaint old days. I think characters like Spence and Lila know all about how hard the past could be. I just had a conversation with my mother this morning. I was asking her when she was growing up in the country in a large household if she had her own spending money. She said no, never, she never had any money. Once she went to the local fair at the school and didn't take anything with her to eat and nobody gave her a nickel to buy a coke or anything and she said the smell of the hamburgers and hot dogs just about starved her to death that day. She married my father when she was seventeen and when they were courting he would take her out to buy hamburgers and cokes. I remember in my own childhood what an incredible experience a hamburger and coke was. I think, by the way, that's why McDonald's is so popular. People have that residual memory of those days in their families, in American history. All those fast foods are basically farm foods—grease and starch. The past is very appealing to a lot of Americans. They see it as something to hold on to, something more cohesive than this fragmented, chaotic life that we mostly live now. But I find the chaos very exciting. People are getting free of a lot of that baggage of the past and I think that's good. I think that people aren't always capable of dealing with change, and yet the possibility of dealing with it is there. I think that's what I was trying to say in the end of "Memphis" [*Love Life*] when Beverly is looking to her future and sees she has choices her parents didn't have. That seems to me an important moment.

Q. Your characters are often enamored of trends and fads. Do you share with them an enthusiasm for what's new?

A. I'm probably more critical of pop culture than most of them, although they're getting more sophisticated all the time and less interested in a lot of garbage. I think I have a sympathetic understanding of why they're watching soap operas or reading the tabloids or whatever they do.

Q. You don't seem to share the impulse of some writers to attack television, to lament the fact that it has replaced reading. In your most recent novel, television brings a harmony into the home of Spence and Lila.

A. Television has brought a lot of outside information and pleasure into people's lives. And whether it's good or bad the fact is that some of my characters feel something for the television programs they watch, feel an affection for the characters in the shows, admire their talent. Now those are real emotions, and we all see things on TV that mean something to us. So I accept that. It used to be that people in a town didn't go out at night, they stayed at home and watched the prime-time line-up. They had their favorite shows. They watched "M*A*S*H" on Saturday nights. Maybe they looked forward to it all day. They had it sort of notched in their skulls that that's what they were going to do. "M*A*S*H" was a very popular program; the final episode was watched by more people than had ever watched any such program before. I think that was culturally significant. The big change now is cable television. There is so much to watch that it all seems empty. I think people have caught on to that. Now they watch movies on their VCR or they go out because there are a lot of things happening since the seventies brought us groups to join. People just seem to be going out more. They're doing more things. They're more athletic, for example.

Q. Is it greater prosperity?

A. I think so.

Q. *In Country* obviously has a lot of references to "**M*A*S*H**." Many of your stories have references to pop culture. Do you ever wonder if twenty-five years from now people will need footnotes?

A. No, I don't worry about it.

Q. You have said, "I feel I'm luckier than some of my characters because I've escaped the circumstances that trapped them. It's an insecure feeling so in a way I feel close to them." Could you talk about the insecure feeling?

A. I feel less threatened now, but I think for a long time I was afraid I might have to get a job in a factory or as an all-night clerk in a motel.

Q. When you left Kentucky, how much of your leaving did you feel was geographical and how much did you feel was cultural or class?

A. Class. Which is bound up with the South and the North, because the South felt so inferior to the North. Southerners react to that sense of inferiority in two ways. One is to stand up fiercely for the South and sing "Dixie" all the time. The other is to reject it and say that the North is the authority and try to learn their ways and get rid of our accents.

Q. Have you made a conscious effort to change your accent?

A. When I went away to school and later to New York to work I made a real conscious effort to lose it, and I virtually did for a long time. Then I realized that was ridiculous, and I tried to regain the natural way of talking.

Q. Recently you've moved back to Kentucky from Pennsylvania. Has coming back had any effects on your writing? Is it any different to write from Kentucky, about Kentucky?

A. I don't know yet. Here's what I imagine, what I think is going to happen; living away for many years, living in the North, I always wrote about Kentucky. Coming back, I think I'm probably going to write about leaving. I'm probably going to send my characters out exploring.

Q. Do you think they'll go north to Pennsylvania?

A. They might. I never wrote about Pennsylvania. I just wasn't motivated. I think the distance gives you a kind of perspective.

Q. So now you think there might be some Pennsylvania stories?
A. Well, only if that's one of the places my characters happen to go. You see, my characters roughly evolve from what's going on in my family. It's not that the fiction is autobiographical, but the family's my source, my anchor, my way of finding out what's going on with people and connecting with the region. In the last few years my family has gotten incredibly scattered. For almost all the time that I was away I was the only one who *was* away, and therefore it was my responsibility to come back, to come home at Christmas, to come home for vacation. Now just in the last few years one sister has moved first to Virginia and then to Florida. Her children have grown up and moved to Virginia and Texas, and one of them has moved from Florida back here and works at the Holiday Inn. And another sister has gotten married and moved to California and is currently in Australia. So it's hard to keep up with them. I find it very disorienting.

Q. Could we discuss a moment the kinds of characters you write about? You said in another context that you see a shift in American writing away from the alienated hero toward characters who are trying to make their way higher into society, into a better position, because they've been down near the bottom. Do you see your own writing in this light? Do you see yourself as departing from classical American fiction with its heroes who typically reject society?
A. I think I did deliberately want to depart from the classics of American fiction in the beginning. Back in graduate school I thought I would like to do that. I tried to do it. I wrote a novel (it was never published) about a twelve-year-old girl, a sort of female Huck Finn. When I was in graduate school I had a wonderful teacher who said all American literature was about the American dream and the American hero who was alienated from American society. He said—this was back in the sixties—in the future, you're going to see a shift, where the hero instead of trying to get *out* of society is trying to get *in*. And of course already that has happened. Much of our fiction now is about marginal people—black literature, Jewish literature, people living on the edge—rather than people who have been in the center and are trying to get out. I have always remembered that my professor said the hero was going to come back in. I didn't know what to make of that, but I thought about it when I started writing about characters who had never been in the center, who had

115

never had that advantage of being able to criticize society enough to leave it, like the hippies were able to do in the sixties.

Q. You once observed that the literary hero of the past typically possesses a "superior sensibility." He is, in effect, an artist, at least emotionally. Your characters may feel things deeply, but they hardly ever strike us as being artistic. They often have trouble expressing themselves. Is there a special challenge in writing about inarticulate people?

A. A character like Spence knows plenty of big words, but he doesn't want to use them.

Q. Why doesn't he want to use them?

A. I don't agree that he can't express himself. I don't think my characters are inarticulate. They do have a vital language, and when they do talk it is quite vigorous. But they are inhibited in their relationships and they don't want to call on verbal ways of communicating. They can talk as well as I can. Certainly as well as I can in an interview. Their reticence is deep-rooted and it goes back generations and grows out of their class and their culture. They don't often know what to say, but that doesn't mean they don't know words. They don't know how to approach the subject or to find the courage to say what they could say, or maybe they don't want to say it because they are stubborn. At the end of "State Champions" [*Love Life*] there is a passage about how country children aren't taught manners, and so they don't say "happy birthday" or "thank you" or things like that. Manners are embarrassing. Verbal communication is very sophisticated and often empty. Saying "thank you" is something you are taught to do to be civilized. For some of my characters, saying "I love you" is a very negative thing, because the meaning is unquestionable and to say it is to commit yourself to a great emotional thing. It is one of those things you don't say. My people don't want to be that revealing about themselves. I said their language is blunt and saying "I love you" would be a very blunt thing to say, but I'm not sure they want to say that. It would be too embarrassing.

Q. It sounds like your characters have two motives for not speaking up. One is a fear of revealing themselves, and the other is pride, a feeling that to say the words is to cheapen the emotion.

A. Yes, and I think that to a character like Spence, a man of country speech, many words might seem comically inappropriate. To use a multisyllabic word that is not usually part of his vocabulary, even though he knows it, would seem like a pretension, and he does not want to put on airs.

Q. You've said, "I feel if I can make characters know far fewer words than I know then I won't be scared of them and I'll be in charge." You were joking, but is there perhaps some truth in the comment? You don't often write about characters who have anywhere near your education. Is it partly a control issue?

A. Oh, I think that's probably it. I think probably I don't have the confidence to write about a lot of things. I would find it hard to write about somebody who has a lot of knowledge about something I don't understand, hard to grasp that person's way of expressing himself.

Q. Most of your audience is, like you, more educated than your characters. Do you picture a particular audience when you write?

A. No, and I find it odd that I'm writing for an audience that is particularly well educated. I'm sorry the general public can't read what I write. I think that they are capable of it, but they don't have access to it. People don't know that they can go to the library and read. I think they feel a class inhibition. There are plenty of things that people who haven't graduated from high school are capable of reading, but their jobs and their worlds prevent them from taking an interest in it. A factory worker is not going to go to the opera. It's just unthinkable. That's not his world, he wouldn't be comfortable. People are taught that things outside their class are inappropriate, and I think that's unfortunate because there are a lot of things that could be of interest to them. I don't think I write fiction that's for a select group.

Q. What sort of reactions have you gotten from people around here about the way you portray them?

A. I haven't heard reactions. I'm not sure a lot of people around here read my work. I should qualify that. I think a lot of people wouldn't *want* to read my work because they might find it too close to their lives. They're not interested in reading something that familiar; it would make them uncomfortable. More have probably read *In Coun-*

try, which sold very widely once it was learned the movie was being made. I think most people are much more interested in the movie.

Q. What do you think it is in your work that would make people uncomfortable?

A. Well, it's not television. It's not fantasy. It's realistic. I think a lot of people just look for escape, Danielle Steele novels, for instance.

Q. You've said, "Letting the imagination loose is a way of getting at stuff that's underneath." Could you give us an example of a particular work where you did that, a breakthrough, when you felt like you got at something underneath?

A. I think I meant that in a more general way. I feel that writer's block is a common state of mind and almost constant for many writers. The act of writing is a battle to get at what's underneath, to break down the barriers to expression. I think writing is a matter of opening up channels to your experience. I feel like mine is pretty far down there, so the act of digging it out is hard.

Q. Why do you think it's so far down there?

A. It's cultural repression and lack of encouragement. I think my experience of going North caused me to repress my own sense of identity and to lose what confidence I had in my own intelligence. I don't even know what I know.

Q. Is there a particular story where you really feel like you got into a vein?

A. No, I was thinking in general about letting loose and getting into an inspired state where you can feel like you're getting something.

Q. What is that inspired state like?

A. It's like you're not conscious of your body and you're kind of flying along in a state of excitement with high energy and a good feeling. Working up to that stage is kind of hard because I have all these physical sensations that prevent it. If I can't get started I realize I'm hungry so then I eat, and then I'm sleepy and I drink coffee, then I feel bad. It's kind of a daily battle. If you can transcend all that, you feel good.

Q. How long do these periods of inspiration last?

A. If I control the coffee and the food just right and get a high energy level, then it could go on for a few hours. And on the best days, really the best times I've ever had, I can write a whole draft of a twenty-page story. That's good.

Q. That's terrific. How often does that happen?
A. It used to happen a lot more often. There's a kind of innocence that goes into it, letting a story fly around like that. Once you do it often enough you get more self-conscious about it and then your vision of what's possible gets more complicated and you place a lot more expectations on yourself. Then it's harder to get that innocent flow, because you start criticizing everything. So I think the writing ability has improved, though the vision of what's possible has become more complicated and so the writing's harder.

Q. How do you handle the bad days, when the writing's not going well?
A. I play at it, and then I give up.

Q. It doesn't affect the rest of your life if you have a bad day writing?
A. I'm not very emotional about it. I don't think about writing when I'm not sitting at the typewriter.

Q. You've been called a minimalist, a dirty realist, a Kmart realist, and so forth. Obviously these labels are more interesting to critics than to writers. But do any of the labels seem more appropriate than the others? And would you yourself distinguish the brand of realism you write? You once called it "hard realism."
A. I guess I used that description not so much as a label as a way of saying my writing is plain or matter-of-fact. I don't know about labels. But I got a kick out of that dirty realist tag. John Barth had one, too, that amused me—a blue-collar hyper-realist super-minimalist, something like that.

Q. Do you think that's accurate?
A. I don't think any label is ever totally accurate.

Q. What about the description of your writing as minimalist?
A. I'm not sure what's meant by minimalism. I'm not sure if it means something that is just so spare that there is hardly anything there, or if it describes something that is deliberately pared down with

great artistic effect, or if it's just a misnomer for what happens in any good short story, which is economy.

Q. Your comments in previous interviews have emphasized style as important to you. You said once, "My favorite writers are those that have a unique style." What do you think your style is like?

A. I try to approximate language that's very blunt and Anglo-Saxon. Instead of saying "a decorative vase of assorted blooms from the garden," I might say "a jug of flowers." "A jug of big red flowers." A lot of it is not just the meaning but the sound of the words and the rhythm of the words and the way they come out of a way of talking. It's also a certain attitude toward the world. Imagine a person who would say "jug" instead of "vase." Style comes out of a way of hearing people talk.

Q. Is your style an approximation of the sounds you have in your head from when you were a child and from the way people around here speak?

A. It's not literally the way they speak. It's something you fashion. It has to do with a kind of projection from inside.

Q. One of the complaints about minimalists is that they take too narrow and personal a view, they don't give us a broad context. In stories like "Detroit Skyline, 1949" and "The Ocean," however, you obviously do provide a historical context. Is this part of your purpose? Do you want us to view your characters as in some sense representative?

A. It just happens. It just turns out that way. I don't know that I typically set out to establish a larger social context for my work. But I did with *In Country*. My editor told me, when I started writing the novel, that the novel in general has a lot broader substance than a short story. Meaning a social context, I think. It has deeper issues. I think I bore that in mind when I was working on it.

Q. You write almost exclusively in the present tense. Did that just happen or did you experiment with it?

A. Actually, I don't think I've written in the present tense in a few years. All the stories in *Shiloh* and most of the stories in *Love Life* are in the present tense. But the ones in the back of *Love Life* are more recent, and they're in past tense. This signaled a change for me. It wasn't a calculated effect. I just wrote in the present tense because it seemed right at the time, I think it was a fashion; it was perfectly appropriate to the times and that's why a lot of people found themselves using it. It obviously came from television, you know. It's very expressive in a way. But I got bored with it. I started seeing it everywhere and it just made me feel like doing something different.

Q. Did you discover the present tense on your own, or did you read another writer using it and think you'd like to try that?
A. Everybody was writing in the present tense. I wouldn't say I copied it but I wouldn't say I originated it either. It was in the air.

Q. Does writing in the present tense prevent your characters from having a sense of the past or an ability to step out of their immediate experience?
A. I think mainly it has to do with the author's authority. If the author is writing in present tense then you get the impression he doesn't know any more than you do about what's happening. You're going along with the author. If the author starts in the past tense, if he says, "Once upon a time," then you assume he has sorted events out, he has a perspective on them, has judged them in some sense. I think the uncertainty of the present tense said a lot about what we were making of the late twentieth century, or were unable to make of it.

Q. But now your stories are primarily in the past tense?
A. One effect of using past tense is that you go along a lot faster. For example, here in the present tense, the phone is ringing. The waitress wants to answer the phone. She picks up the phone. "Hello," she says. You could get bogged down for days . . . and you can't skip large chunks of time. You can't say she answers the phone today and then say it is three weeks later. How did that consciousness skip all that time? Who's doing the plotting? Who's behind the camera?

Q. Ann Beattie once said that writing in present tense helped her to imagine everything happening.
A. Yes, that sense of immediacy is very valuable. And also, there's that habit people have, when they tell a story: "So I go . . . then, he goes. . . ." The present tense is a natural storytelling mode. You turn it on and you go.

Q. There are at least a couple of stories in *Love Life* where you do unusual things with point of view. Unusual for short stories, that is.

A. You mean like two different points of view?

Q. There's the shifting third-person point of view in the title story "Love Life." And the first- and third-person points of view in "Marita," which is even more unusual.

A. Also, in "Marita," I shift between present and past tense.

Q. What was behind that, or do you remember?

A. No, I don't remember. I'm sure it just developed. I can't imagine that I sat down and said, now I'm going to experiment with point of view and tense. It was a revelation for me to have hit upon the alternating points of view in "Love Life" because I'd never tried such a thing before. It seemed to make a breakthrough, force some shift. That story was written before *Spence + Lila*, in which I did the same thing.

Q. What about the two different points of view and the shifts between past and present tense in "Marita"?

A. It felt very interesting writing it that way. I tend to write by piecing things together, and it may very well be that I looked at different fragments and then just somehow put them together.

Q. That story is about an abortion, a critical decision. Are the different points of view and tenses perhaps supposed to emphasize the gap between the mother's feelings and the daughter's?

A. The daughter is the one experiencing it in the present and the one who's feeling it, so the first person, present tense seems to work more for that, but the mother has more critical distance, and third person, past tense seems to fit for her. That's the way I feel about it anyway.

Q. You published a book on Nabokov [*Nabokov's Garden: A Guide to "Ada,"* 1974] and have talked about having a strange affinity with Nabokov's sensibility. How would you describe his sensibility?

A. I think his extraordinary childhood allowed him to indulge a child's way of seeing that's up close and particular. What I admire about Nabokov's work are his details and his seizing on the tiniest things. He thought these were the essence of reality, things you wouldn't notice necessarily. Nabokov said that the literal meaning is so much more important than what people find underlying it. He was much more interested in the pattern of the butterfly wing than in anything about symbolism or life on the wing or whatever butterflies are supposed to represent.

Q. Do you think that's true of your work?

A. Obviously, my writing is nothing like his, but details and images can radiate and shimmer and evoke emotions. Whereas, if you talk about a story as showing a contrast between, say, the old and the new ways of life or as being about the New South, well, either that's very obvious or it is something I never even thought of. I have difficulty with abstractions, with questions about themes. I think that when you teach literature that's what you're dealing with a lot of times, because students want to know what it means. There was an article about "Shiloh," which reduced it all to these generalizations, and I felt like it was all very efficiently abstracted, so why did I go to all the trouble to write it as a story? Maybe most students are at an age where qualities and textures don't make much sense. When Nabokov taught modern European literature he typically gave his students exams with factual questions, like what was the color of Madame Bovary's dress, what color were Anna Karenina's eyes. He said he wanted them to read the work so thoroughly that they would remember even those details. I think that's a good approach. Writing is like making a quilt. You spend weeks and weeks doing all these intricate stitches and intricate patterns and colors. And then you finish it and somebody says, "Oh, this is about the Civil War." A total surprise! Abstractions have their place, of course, even for writers. I just kind of make up these terms that I use when I'm looking at my fiction critically to see if it's working. Things like balance and tone and emotional center and emotional direction, continuity, weight. Then somewhere along the way I'll discover what it's about or where the center is. But rarely am I able to reduce it to its meaning.

Q. Something else you said about Nabokov was that you like the way he celebrates life.

A. He was the most positive writer; everything was just full of joy for him and he wanted to be intensely alive every second.

Q. In *Lolita* isn't the world ugly and unfinished and accidental? Doesn't it require the artist's vision to redeem it?

Part 2

A. Well, that may be true in the fiction. Some people think of Nabokov as a very aristocratic, snobbish sort of writer who looks down on anything crude and unformed and limited. I guess I'm influenced by what I read about him as a person and get that confused with his work. But I can see in his work the joy he took in the artistry and so I want to apply what I read about him as a person. By his own statements, the only things that he truly rejected and truly hated were deliberate cruelty and totalitarianism. I don't think he looked down on people. His whole background was very democratic and liberal, and I don't think he dismissed the human race. I think his critics also confuse the life with the work.

Q. Do you think you also celebrate life in your fiction?
A. Oh, well, yeah, I'd like to think that. I can't believe anybody actually celebrates life every second. But I think I essentially have a positive view of things. I think Nabokov had a comic vision and I think that means celebratory.

Q. Any theories about why *Shiloh* was such a success?
A. All I know is that people did tell me it struck a chord, and very often it was people who were transplanted from small towns and rural backgrounds. It seemed to ring a bell and remind people of something they've tried to get away from. As I have.

Q. Is "Detroit Skyline, 1949" autobiographical?
A. It's not autobiographical; it's inspired by one little memory and two or three details, the memory being that I went on a trip to Michigan with my mother when I was nine and saw my first television set. I remember the buses were on strike and we couldn't go into downtown Detroit. And that's just about all I remember. I wanted to write about somebody encountering television for the first time. I was thinking about what that meant. Anyway, I got hold of the *Detroit Free Press* for that period and I found the bus strike and I also found the Red Scare, which got me real interested. So I collected a lot of information from the newspapers.

Q. What differences do you see between the two collections of stories [*Shiloh* and *Love Life*]?
A. I think the characters' world changed a good bit between the two. I think life was changing so fast that they got more sophisticated,

124

they've gotten more mobile, and I'd like to think that the stories have gotten more complex. I think my characters' lives were a lot simpler in the first collection.

Q. Do you think the changes in tense and point of view in the second collection are related to the stories' greater complexity?

A. I'd like to think that.

Q. When you take individual stories and put them in a collection, do you just compile what you think are your best stories at the time, or do you try to shape them into a unified whole?

A. I try not to put two stories that are very much alike right next to each other. In *Love Life*, I began with a story about an old person and ended it with old people, and I think I had the more recent stories in the past tense toward the end because I felt that moved things in a forward direction. "Bumblebees" was the central story that it all radiated from. I had a complicated scheme that I can't quite remember now. It was very organic. Maybe you can figure that out.

Q. I really liked the story "Midnight Magic" in the second collection. One of the amazing things about it is that even though its protagonist is unintelligent and insensitive, we end up liking him, caring about him.

A. That story was inspired by a guy I saw sitting in a car eating chocolate-covered doughnuts and drinking chocolate milk. He looked like he had a hangover and felt horrible. He looked like a really mean person and I wondered about him, so I started writing a story. While I was writing it I couldn't make the person I had seen follow through in my imagination. The real person looked like he could be a rapist and really mean. But I couldn't write him that way. I made him a whole lot nicer than I thought he would be, and I kept thinking he was too nice. I had to explore, and I don't know why he came out the way he did other than, as I said, I kept trying to tone him down. I think we've all seen thousands of people who don't have any sense of responsibility but they want to be liked, they want to do right. They want to be in love and they want to make people happy. They just can't bring themselves to put forth the effort. They're just totally out of control.

Q. In your stories religion is not very often a source of strength and solace for your characters, which seems a little surprising since they live in the Bible Belt. Can you comment on why that is?

A. It's just a failing on my part. I haven't written much about religion, just like I haven't really written about any black characters. Religion is just not a part of many of my characters' lives. I've tried just to refer to it in passing, to make it a normal part of their lives in some cases. But I don't feel confident about approaching religion. I think it's a tricky subject. I do try to think about religion, and I'm real interested in the evangelists and what effects they've had on people. I even went to Heritage U.S.A. to look around for inspiration for a story. I just haven't been able to write it.

Q. Why is religion a tricky subject? Is it the difficulty of capturing the religious sensibility itself, or is it the fear of seeming to belittle or make fun of people's beliefs?

A. I think that it's hard to do seriously and delicately, and I don't know how to do it from the inside. One of these days I'll work on it.

• • •

Q. Recently you said that you had more sympathy for the men in the stories, that women seemed to be breaking through, finding new opportunities, and the men seemed to have lost their way.

A. That goes back to "Shiloh." I didn't have any worries about Norma Jean, but Leroy was quite bewildered by all the change.

• • •

Q. When I teach "Shiloh" many of the women students assume it's Norma Jean's story and cheer her on for trying to take control and move out of her confining background. They overlook Leroy and don't recognize that it's his story, told from his point of view. Is that common?

A. Not uncommon. And you can imagine my surprise when I hear that some students think Norma Jean is going to jump because she's standing on the edge of a cliff at the end of the story. That's so weird. Maybe *Leroy* would jump but not Norma Jean. She's a survivor.

• • •

Q. Just as you bring new kinds of characters to our attention, aren't you also validating certain positive feelings that aren't very prominent in contemporary writing?

A. I think my stories tend to end at a moment of illumination, and I think that in itself is hopeful. For example, Leroy in "Shiloh" recognizes that his life has got to change. His situation is difficult, but he now knows he can't just deny it or ignore it, and I think that knowledge is hopeful. I see the excitement of possibility for a lot of my characters at the end of their stories. At the end of "Love Life" and "Wish" and "Memphis," for example, I'm really thrilled at what the characters can remember and can conceive in their imaginations.

An Interview with Bobbie Ann Mason
Albert Wilhelm

Q. How have your early experiences influenced your writing?

A. When I was growing up, there were two pastimes that were most important in shaping my literary direction. One was my early obsession with jigsaw puzzles. I loved to work puzzles, and all the women in my family still do. We love putting together the colors and patterns and seeing the full design emerge. It's thrilling and satisfying, especially discovering that the most unlikely piece belongs. Second, I helped my grandmother piece quilts, and that was another version of working a puzzle. These childhood loves are probably my strongest early artistic sources.

And so I loved words, which are bits of language you can piece together to make stories. I was always fascinated by words. New words were little mysteries, sounds without meanings, tunes that caught in my brain insistently. My favorite course in high school was Latin, and then I took French in college. To my regret, I didn't learn to speak it. When I went to France, I thought I had never heard such a beautiful language. In college I took a course in etymology, and I wrote columns for the school newspaper in which I got to indulge my fondness for word play. My friends and I would read Shakespeare and go around saying "Hark!" and "Prithee!" because we thought they were funny things to say. From *Cyrano de Bergerac,* I think, we got "magnolious" and "magnelephant," words we dearly loved and used continually. In graduate school my first course was Old English, which had wonderful words like "upgang" and "langung." My husband and I named our first dog "Beowulf."

Q. What writers influenced you?

A. As a child, I loved Louisa May Alcott. But I didn't turn on to any other writers until I was in college. When I was a freshman, I was passionate about Thomas Wolfe. After that, it was F. Scott Fitzgerald, and then Salinger.

This interview took place in Nashville, Tennessee, on 15 October 1995.

128

In graduate school I discovered James Joyce and Vladimir Nabokov. I would say they are the principal writers who influenced me, even though I don't write at all like them (and I certainly don't claim to be in their league). But it was the sense of what could be done with language that dazzled me. The possibilities were endless. A writer could arrange words to suggest the most complicated feelings and visions. I admired stylists, the ones who found the most interesting and pleasing ways of getting at the deepest matters. In the best ones, form and content were inseparable.

I had not read widely and I was not very sophisticated about anything. As a student, I had been for the most part looking for answers and intellectual systems and ideas and didn't have much of a sense of aesthetics. So the academic discipline of graduate school didn't inhibit my creative spirit, as so many writers complain. Just the opposite. I had been trained all my life to memorize lessons and not ask questions. So the discovery of what creative minds had done was an awakening—probably something that happens to most writers long before they encounter graduate school. Somehow I didn't catch on to the competitive career goals of graduate school or to critical methodology. I was more caught up in the literature itself. It was thrilling, because it was so complicated and detailed, like a million-piece puzzle with an elusive design—but much, much more. Through the music of language in Joyce and Nabokov, I discovered how literature could both embody and also transcend ideas. Literature is principally about textures and feelings, not themes and symbols, which are sort of like lead weights on the bottom of a shower curtain. They hold it in place and give it shape, but they aren't the curtain itself.

Q. How did you get from that point to your own concerns about place—your persistent focus on small towns in western Kentucky?

A. My artistic interests and influences had nowhere to go for a while, until I could get clear in my mind what I valued most and what my passions were. The artistry is what you bring to bear on the raw material that's foremost in your mind and heart. The art is what you use to work this into shape.

Eventually, after graduate school, I had enough distance from the place I had come from to realize that the language of my family and region was a rich resource, rather than something I took for granted and even wanted to get away from for a time. So that language led me into discovering the place and its people as real materials for fiction.

And by then I began to realize that the place of my origins—my little literary turf of western Kentucky—called to me because that's where my heart and soul are, what I love most. So it's natural for me to want to tell the story of that place and not the story of, say, Boise, Idaho (although ultimately what's true in one small place is true everywhere). Write what you know—the old bromide is true.

The journey I've been on is a common enough one. First, you go out into the world in quest of understanding. Then you return to your origins and finally comprehend them. It wasn't until I had pursued my education that I was able to know where the subject of my fiction was. Education has a way of being abstract until you can link it up with experience. I loved the abstractions, but then at some point, I planted a garden, and everything started to come together. Life, art, cats, family, fiction, words, weeds.

When I finally did "come home" in this sense, I realized how haunted I've always been by the lives of the people I grew up among. The history of western Kentucky is rich and in many ways literally central to American history. It resonates for me—not as something abstract, but as something very concrete and real, in the lives of the people of the area. Their experiences are what I try to capture in my characters. I feel very close to them. My forebears came to this area several generations ago, so my roots here run deep, and I think I know the people here. What I write about essentially is culture shock—the bewildering experience of moving from the land into modern urban life. Culture shock has been my experience, in moving from the South to the North, and I see versions of it in everybody at home as they deal with change. My characters live in a place where generations ago the American dream was actually accomplished, through hardship and sacrifice and adventure—as well as the familiar crimes of the frontier. It was the dream of land and freedom. But in this century, the shift from the independence of rural life is a profound upheaval. Now many people are likely to punch time clocks, while their grandparents would have told time by the sun. People are being redefined as working class, which is a reduction in status, for the yeoman farmer was his own boss. It was a whole different way of life, and the transformation is emotionally complicated.

Q. You described the language of your region and family as a rich resource. Can you say more about how language functions in your writing?

A. Early on, I discovered the significance of tone—how language sounds, what attitude comes through. The sound of words is related to music, and although I really don't know very much about music, I have an ear for the way characters talk. I find music and poetry in the *plainest* of language. I think sometimes the qualities are too slight for some readers to notice or care about, especially if they are not familiar with Southern dialects. But I hear these nuances and work on whether a phrase should end in two syllables or three syllables, for example. My early short-story period was so exciting for me—I was busting out of school and finding out what I could do on my own. I was claiming my imagination and enjoying being playful and bold. My best stories of that period came out of sudden bursts of creative energy that I would then work on endlessly to refine and shape. So basically, in school I discovered literature and then I went out to see if I could do it. It was a shock. Even though I'd read *Moby Dick* and *Ulysses* and many other great works, I found out that in writing you have to start from scratch.

Q. In an introduction to one of the many reprintings of "Shiloh" [in *American Voices*], you describe the creative process as "the not knowing that leads you to the knowing." Can you elaborate?

A. I don't know in advance what I'm going to write, so the process of writing is a way of finding out what's on my mind. I experience writing as a process of digging through writer's block, or the inhibitions that prevent me from getting access to my resources. You can't get at these things through intellectual procedure. And I find that I am guided first by the subject matter, not by artistic method or intention. Form follows function? Sometimes you don't even realize what you've dredged out of the unconscious. It's delightful later to discover patterns and parallels that you didn't consciously realize were in the work. Sometimes they have to be pointed out for me by readers.

Q. Can you comment further on your affinity with Nabokov, the subject of your doctoral dissertation?

A. The reasons I felt drawn to Nabokov go beyond his style. It was the way he used words to tone down and contain and hold at a distance emotions so strong that they would otherwise blubber all over the page. The artistry of that containment, and those diversionary tactics he used, created a powerful tension between the conscious mind and the world. Also, I was interested in how he refused to reduce everything to two levels—a symbolic level and an underlying significance. He saw that everything was on the surface level, but that it is so infinitely complex that it radiates and shimmers into some kind of transcendence. Reality is like a kaleidoscope. Each facet has its own reality, and how you see it depends on where you are standing. So there are infinite ways of looking. For Nabokov, the scientist and the artist have the best chances of escaping this subjective prison. Nabokov wasn't satisfied with the appearance/reality division of Western thought. As a Southerner, I know that appearances *are* reality. So I found Nabokov's vision very appealing, especially his imagery of sun and shade, light and shadow. He would play with the mingling of those images endlessly, it seems. There is not simply light and dark, good and evil. But they are mingled, flickering, casting shadows and flashes. "Dappling" was his favorite word for the play of light against dark. It seems to me that chaos theory, which has come along recently, is perfectly suited to Nabokov's grasp of the universe. Chaos is a misnomer, because within the seeming chaos there are extraordinary patterns—paisleys mostly, it seems, to judge by the computer models. Nabokov's way of seeing the world is like a dynamic, reflecting patchwork quilt, and I find that view very exciting. I love the notion of chaos, with the uncertainties it implies, because it holds the challenge of discovering something new, some pieces that fit together in startling ways.

Q. So the image patterns in your stories could be analogous to the patterns of shape and color in a complicated quilt?

A. I guess so. I never consciously thought of this quilt business when I was writing the early stories. In retrospect, this is one of the metaphors I have discovered for articulating my original sources. I'm most attracted to the crazy quilts, which seem closer to chaos theory. But most of my early training was regimented—coloring books, neat little quilt blocks, following the rules at school, and so forth. So it has been important for me to get beyond those limits. I'm not especially interested in quilts, actually, and it has been a long time since I tackled a coloring book.

Q. Did living away from your native region enable you to write about it more perceptively? How has your recent move back to Kentucky altered your perception of your fictional materials?

A. During my years in the Northeast, I was able to develop a perspective I would not have had if I had stayed home. That's a common enough experience. Being an exile seemed to give the place more importance as an inspiration and an impetus for writing.

Now that I'm back in Kentucky, it's no longer that place I come home to. It's where I live, and so I may risk losing some of the perspective I've had. But, on the other hand, I needed a closer familiarity with what is going on in Kentucky now, since I had found it necessary to write about the place. After I moved back, I became preoccupied with the historical forces that shaped the world I'm from. Those interests culminated in the novel *Feather Crowns*, and even though I finished that some time ago I'm still preoccupied with the history of the people and the place. Since I began writing contemporary short stories set in this place, it has changed so rapidly that I may have to turn a sharp corner into the unknown in future stories.

Q. Is delving further back into local history a way of reestablishing roots?

A. Only a strongly rooted person would celebrate chaos! There was never any question about my roots or where they were. It's not that I felt dislocated. It's a matter of curiosity, of going deeper into those roots, digging them up, so to speak. Growing up in the country on a farm, which was on the edge of town, I was rooted but heading out in all directions. I felt confident in leaving because I was pretty sure of where home was. It had been there for generations, and there was no chance of it disappearing. Actually, my motive for delving into the past is an overwhelming curiosity to find out what-all went into the stew we live in. In moving back to Kentucky, I had to take this route, to get my bearings. Maybe that's what you asked.

Q. And a short story doesn't allow enough scope for all that? Is that why you have concentrated lately on novels?

A. That might be the case. I don't categorize my interests quite that way. The boundaries blur. Fiction and nonfiction blend. Stories and novels. Sun and shade. The early stories were surprises. I enjoy thinking and remembering the excitement of discovery, the workings of the imagination, how those stories seemed to come out of

133

nowhere and to be delightful and puzzling at the same time. To write them one after the other and not ask why, just let them come alive and work on them until they seemed right. It was a joyous experience, but writing a few stories is less rewarding in the long run than writing a novel.

Q. In contrast to many early stories with very contemporary settings, your writing now involves more research into historical materials?

A. I'm not sure what that has to do with my writing. It's an infusion, a way of figuring out things about the world. I'm compelled to ask questions and to expand my understanding about how the world works and to bring everything I can to bear upon the fundamental concerns about our place in the universe. The raw material is the language and landscape of a particular place, but by using those personal and particular terms I hope to create a new place—a simpler one in a way but one that has carefully chosen furnishings and a lively, unexpected center of action. Writing is a way of delving into your buried resources—the turbulence of experience—and coming up with shapes, patterns, stories. All those dazzling pieces waiting to fall into place.

Part 3

THE CRITICS

Introduction

As the bibliography for this volume indicates, the critical essays on Mason's short fiction are still relatively few in number, but their approaches are highly varied. An early essay by Edwin T. Arnold focuses on Mason's treatment of the modern family while articles by Tina Bucher and G. O. Morphew examine Mason's "downhome feminism." In two very different essays Robert H. Brinkmeyer Jr. analyzes Mason's use of contemporary music as well as her roots in Southern traditions. As a further exploration of Mason's Southern heritage, Darlene Reimers Hill writes about the importance of food and food rituals within the stories. An essay by Linda Adams Barnes points out parallels with the work of Flannery O'Connor, and one by Barbara Henning compares minimalist stories by Mason and Raymond Carver. The essays reprinted here by Richard Giannone and Leslie White exemplify this variety and provide valuable insights on individual stories.

Some readers have been preoccupied with (or occasionally repulsed by) the surface details of Mason's stories—her numerous references to Kmart, Donahue, and Elvis. Giannone acknowledges the importance of these references but moves deftly beyond such phenomena to examine an important metaphysical core. He argues that Mason's stories about separation, illness, and death are much more than accurate chronicles of contemporary society because they offer a vision of "the distant, unseen dimension of life." Giannone provides detailed analysis of three stories that embody this vision.

White's essay focuses squarely on Mason's pervasive allusions to popular culture and asks what such allusions contribute to the narratives. She argues that in *Shiloh and Other Stories* popular culture tends to isolate or tranquilize characters while in *In Country* it becomes "a means of continuity and communication."

Richard Giannone

These are at once dispiriting times and revelatory days for the women and men of western Kentucky who people the stories of Bobbie Ann Mason. The heroine of "Third Monday," Ruby Jane MacPherson, expresses the moral mood when she says with dark and knowing nonchalance that "The twentieth century's taking all the mysteries out of life" (232). The secrets that Ruby believes are being eliminated do not concern esoteric phenomena set high above the earth or God's dealings with humankind through inscrutable laws. Rather, Ruby has in mind the obscurities concealed within everyday living that we forbear through disregard but must take into account when recognition of them is forced on us by the swift scientific or cultural advancements of our era. Whereas ignorance of separation, illness, and death allows for hope, the unveiling of submerged realities can instill dread. The contingencies in Mason's story vary in nature and import with the characters' plight, but throughout her writing the mysteries are something personal, sharply felt by the body if incomprehensible to the mind, and intensely alive. And though the disclosures upset all the peace that the characters have been trusting for years, the crisis opens them up to a new unknown, an untried inner resource that might take them beyond dashed equanimity.

With Ruby it is the appearance of a lump in her breast that subverts a previously unalloyed confidence in her body, a young, lovely body that without warning betrays her by harboring a furtive energy beyond her control. Once begun, the shattering gains technological speed. Mammography flattens Ruby's curvaceous breast into X-ray lines "on Xerox paper." A diagnosis of malignancy leads to a radical mastectomy; chemotherapy and radiation may ensue. The cumulative threat of modern medicine is to eradicate Ruby's inmost definition of herself—the feeling of female wholeness that she takes for granted as the basis of her relation with herself, her lover, and her rural Kentucky world. Her shapeliness manifests her integrity. Mystery for Ruby is her irreducible humanness.

"Bobbie Ann Mason and the Recovery of Mystery," from *Studies in Short Fiction* 27 (Fall 1990): 553–66. © 1990 by Newberry College. Reprinted by permission.

Her recent awareness that it can be unaccountably imperiled underlies Ruby's disquiet about the demystifying tenor of our century.

Ruby finds a sympathetic audience in Linda, a friend to whom she makes the comment. Both women have need for a gratifying surprise. Linda is thirty-seven, pregnant, unmarried, and resolved not to marry the out-of-towner who fathered her baby. Amniocentesis determines the child's sex and informs Linda that her daughter's chromosomal balance is normal. Given the risks of pregnancy at Linda's age and the hardship awaiting her as a working single parent, the disclosures of genetic screening are reassuring enough for Linda to name her unborn daughter Holly. But medical science also deprives this expectant mother of felt wonder by reducing the awesomeness of childbirth to physiological anticlimax. Glad as Linda is that her baby will be a healthy girl, she still feels cheated of experiencing the inviolate life-giving power of her body. "But in a way," Linda submits to her friends, knowing about Holly before Holly arrives is "like knowing ahead of time what you're going to get for Christmas" (232).

Linda and Ruby define the predicament pervading Bobbie Ann Mason's stories. Her rural characters are caught between an incomprehensible other-worldly force and the actual loss sustained by their this-worldly anguish. Their suffering cuts two ways. All are mystified by contemporary life at the same time that they are robbed of the mysteries of their lives. Mason's Kentuckians grapple with their bewilderment to find the source of their lives, the joyous mystery of being alive, the Christmas gift of marvel that Linda seeks and tries to preserve by naming Holly for the holiday excitement she does not want to lose. Such fundamental desires are the mysteries that our vexing age discounts, and they are the mysteries that Bobbie Ann Mason in her stories sets out to recover. She does so by relying on the appeal in the very physical distress besetting her characters to raise their moral imagination to the possibility of fuller life.

Mason's writing commanded attention when *Shiloh and Other Stories*, her first collection, appeared in 1982. In the span of a few years that critical interest has deepened. One contributor to *Since Flannery O'Connor: Essays on the Contemporary American Short Story* (1987) aligns Mason's portrayal of emotional and bodily disfigurement with the tradition of Southern grotesque, and goes so far as to identify Mason as heiress to O'Connor's legacy (Barnes 133–41). If O'Connor's theological handling of physical deformity and her eschatological extension of mystery prove to exceed Mason's deliberate cultural focus, as I think they will, their shared involvement with rural Southernness will certainly provide a source of consideration.[1] In fact, one reader already has initiated the discussion by proposing that Mason charts "a new direction for the Southern renascence" in her adaption of history to understand the disarray of contemporary experience (Brinkmeyer 21).

The power of Mason's writing does lie in her insight into our historical and cultural dislocations, but she is more than an astute chronicler of how we live now. She is alive to the distant, unseen dimension of life. One way into her art is to see how her characters, who are lost amid the Burger Chefs, Kmarts, and television talk shows that level western Kentucky into the nondescript American landscape, find their spiritual portion in the turmoil. Since inaugural criticism is most useful when anchored in particulars, this essay offers an introduction to Mason's distinguishing strength through readings of three stories: "Shiloh," "The Retreat," and "Third Monday." These are arguably the best of the sixteen comprising *Shiloh and Other Stories*. Mason herself gives prominence to "Shiloh" by designating it the title story, and assigns "Third Monday" the privilege of bringing the sequence to a close. "The Retreat" puts into relief the importance of gender in coping with trauma. Together the stories exemplify Mason's subject and vision.

The larger themes in the stories arise from the breakdown in intimacy. A spouse or lover tries to shatter the bonds tied by love and strained by a medical problem. Whether the struggle in one partner is for release or in another for reconciliation, the outcome is a painful awareness of aloneness that occasions a new response, a momentary self-communication about the heart's desire for freedom.

"Shiloh" begins with Norma Jean Moffitt developing her pectorals with three-pound dumbbells as a warm-up for a twenty-pound barbell. She wants to gain the strength in her muscles that will prime her spirit. Accordingly, she also has a workout for her mind. While spare daytime hours go to firming up the contour of her chest, evenings are devoted to outlining paragraphs for her classes at Paducah Community College. Norma Jean has the idea of female independence in search of a body to flesh it out and of a mental fitness to assert it. Although the reader may smile at Wonder Woman's attempt to shape her inner life by means of cultural formulas, Mason respects the struggle for autonomy, and through the events of the story gauges its effect on Norma Jean's marriage to Leroy.

Leroy Moffitt, thirty-four, is a truckdriver. "Shiloh" is his story. Four months before the story begins, his tractor-trailer jackknifed in Missouri, leaving him with a mangled leg fastened by a steel pin. The world of Leroy the king is racked by crisis. His driving days are over. His rig sits in the backyard; Leroy sits on the couch smoking marijuana—two huge birds roosting at home. Miniature instruments of power, such as a model B-17 and a truck, replace the machine he cannot operate. Toys not only allow vicarious control over the engine that crippled him; they also serve as a holding action against thoughts about a more obscure mechanism that he feels keeps him disabled. Handicrafts bring out the trucker's delicate side as he becomes adroit at string art, macrame, and needlepoint. As male traits mark Norma Jean's move toward independence, female qualities underscore Leroy's effort to regain power. The feminine side of Leroy becomes so pronounced that his mother-in-law, Mabel Beasley, mocks him.

Mason, however, does not set the idea of femininity against the idea of masculinity. Rather, her treatment of gender points up her concern for totality. Norma Jean's body-building and Leroy's model-building derive from the same basic need to complete oneself. She needs male strength to transform her life, and he needs female insight to change his life. The new androgynous tone in their relationship suggests that the way to rebuild their marriage is by experiencing the other's vulnerability and by developing the other's complementary skill. Mystery lies in the totality of humanness that both seek by virtue of their painful sense of partiality.

Leroy welcomes a fresh start. Now that he is disabled, he realizes "that in all the years he was on the road he never took time to examine anything" (2). He loves Norma Jean, believes that his marriage has a future, and wants intimacy. This bruiser is not afraid of tenderness. When Norma Jean becomes edgy about his idleness, Leroy does not cover exposure with anger. Nor does he impose his sexual desire on her. He accepts the cool morning place in bed that Norma Jean leaves after disappearing to sell cosmetics at Rexall's. During the lonely years on the highway, Leroy would tell hitchhikers his life story; now, at home and alone in his marriage, he wants to express himself to Norma Jean, "as if he had just met her" (9).

Two plans unfold for Leroy and Norma Jean to reacquaint themselves. Both fail. The first is Leroy's idea to build a log house, "a real home" (7), to lay a foundation for a new life. The dream house gives the grown man a way out of confinement. His maternal instinct for a hearth kindles a feeling of being physically strong and emotionally open. Lincoln logs will provide a refuge from danger and drabness; simplicity will promote healing. The mail-order blueprints covering the table, how-ever, limn a pie in the sky. This twentieth-century idea of how the nine-teenth century ought to have been in rural Kentucky cannot bring the security Leroy wants. For one thing, Norma Jean has a contemporary notion of how she wants to live her life; but more ruinous are the struc-tural weaknesses in his conception of the log house. The blueprint is for a shell. Emotions, not Leroy's imaginary timber, build closeness.

The second plan is Mabel Beasley's. Her latest interference in the marriage of Norma Jean and Leroy is to propose a second honeymoon in Shiloh. Shiloh for these Southerners has nothing to do with the Civil War; it is Mabel's cure-all for marital ills. Not surprisingly, the Sunday trip to southwestern Tennessee does not work magic in Norma Jean and Leroy. The national park at Pittsburg Landing to the weary couple is just another place that takes a long drive to reach. The setting bores them. Natural changes over 120 years, enhanced by diligent park atten-dants, have altered the battleground of one of the bloodiest slaughters on American soil into a neat, immense subdivision. Time and grooming alone do not deprive Shiloh of meaning. Dispossession lies in Leroy and Norma Jean. The act of the mind that brings the past to bear on the present is not part of the Moffitts' post-Vietnam sensibility. Leroy expects a golf course and thinks of the dead soldiers whose markers sur-round him as "a board game with plastic soldiers" (15). Dissociation cramps Leroy's response to historical catastrophe as well as to marital crisis: he turns suffering into an idea and reacts to the abstraction. He needs a blueprint to deal with the woman he loves. As for Norma Jean, at Shiloh she remains emotionally elsewhere, perhaps lost in the unnamed "book about another century" (13) that absorbed her the evening Leroy badgered her to visit Shiloh.

Since the mind holds no refuge from pain, Leroy and Norma Jean can no more avoid the anguish of separation than the Confederate and Union troops before them could escape each other's gunfire. The second honey-mooners enact their private battle. "I want to leave you," Norma Jean declares. Shocked, Leroy slumps on the grass, his stoned mind useless in grasping the blow he receives. Finally, he comes back, "No, you don't," and the fight unfolds like a lyric for country blues awaiting Elvis or Chuck Berry to back up the pain with melody. Norma Jean, in the end, can and will be cruel to a heart that's true, and Leroy has neither the power to stop her nor the words to express his hurting impotence.

But Mason's hero does have the capacity to intuit the pattern of human affairs. Jet Beasley and Mabel married and honeymooned in

Shiloh, then Norma Jean was born, and then Jet died. Then Leroy and Norma Jean married, had a baby named Randy, and Randy died of crib death, and now Norma Jean is pulling away. Leroy perceives that love involves separation, a loss having nothing to do with right or wrong. In Mason's world dispersion just happens. By recalling the cycle of engagement and death in the Confederate and Union forces and in his family, Leroy comes to realize that he "is leaving out the insides of history" just as "the real workings of a marriage" (16) escape him. Without the felt life of history, both his and that of others, Leroy remains caught in a discrete, hollow shell of time. To dramatize the trap of being separated from a temporal context, Mason tells Leroy's story in the vivid present and suspends his plight in irresolution.

Leroy's attempt to love and live apart from the inner workings of love is, like his marijuana smoking, a way of avoiding pain. The outcome is self-absorption, the recognition of which points to a possible release. Earlier in the story, Leroy observes goldfinches flying by the window feeder: "They close their wings, then fall, then spread their wings to catch and lift themselves" (7). And so with Leroy Moffitt. After the crash in Missouri, his energy bounces up with the plan to build a log house, a hope razed by Norma Jean's anger. At the end, her announcement that she wants to leave him brings Leroy still lower. Still, battered but not diminished, Leroy "gets up" (16) from the ground to retrieve Norma Jean at the river where she turns toward him, waving her arms. It is unclear whether she is exercising her chest muscles to flex her power or she is beckoning Leroy. The ambiguity of her gesture does not matter to Leroy. What counts is his getting up and going to her. The goldfinch impulse spreads its wings in Leroy to lift him anew. That life-furthering power that is in the air and in the goldfinch and in Norma Jean's desire for freedom also draws Leroy's disordered affections up into its current. "Shiloh" brings Leroy from accidental collapse to inexplicable ascent.

"The Retreat" depicts a marriage that would seem immune to the disruption vexing Leroy and Norma Jean. Georgeann and Shelby Pickett are married ten years, have two children, and rarely quarrel. Sacrifice to high purpose binds their partnership. Shelby works weekdays as an electrician to support his calling to be a preacher at the Grace United Methodist Church, a dying rural congregation in western Kentucky. Georgeann helps out by typing weekly bulletins, playing the piano at the worship, and performing other tasks expected of a minister's wife. She serves so that he can serve the ministry. The Picketts' life, in fine, goes by the book, just as Leroy wanted his marriage to run. But Georgeann is unhappy. Unable to pinpoint the trouble, she complains of vague rules that "come out of nowhere" (133). Spite is the woman's only defense against the shadowy menace. One Sunday she reacts to an altercation with Shelby by putting on jeans to clean the henhouse. The picture of a preacher's wife carting manure to the garden on the Lord's Day gratifies her need to flout the rules hemming her in. When she finds a sick hen, she belatedly battles Shelby's patronizing indifference to her feelings by repeating his scorn to the droopy hen. Although symbolic rebuke brings Georgeann no satisfaction, Mason respects the petty ill will of a woman trying to break through the cultural pressures the heroine does not grasp.

All Georgeann gets from shoveling manure is dermatosis on her stomach. When the irritations turn out not to be benign chicken mites, as she assumes, but body lice, Georgeann enjoys researching the disease and announcing to Shelby, "I've got lice" (140). If viewed apart from her suppressed anger, Georgeann's fascination with parasites would be morbid; but as a form of protest, pathology makes sense. Attention to a medical problem takes precedence over the countless priorities set by Shelby that rule her life. There is a certain soundness in her being frank about a disease that disgusts others. Georgeann's irrational joy in physical ailment and therapy is her way of reclaiming her body as alive and personal from a husband whose emotions are shaped by rules and from a culture whose values disparage the physical.

Shelby is not the enemy. Georgeann means it when she says that "he's sweet as can be" (143). His benevolence, unfortunately, embodies a rigid dependence on mind that Georgeann is growing away from. With Shelby, reaching out for goodness evaporates into gnostic yearning. He supplies euphemism for plain action, as when the children take long baths as a precaution against lice and he speaks of "a ritual cleansing, something like baptism" (141). Ten years of such fervor give a disembodied aura to his and Georgeann's intimacy.

The flashpoint for Georgeann's distress is the annual retreat at Kentucky Lake that delighted her for years and now upsets her. Here we see the essential opponent. The retreat in "The Retreat" is a flight from the physical that reinforces an individual identity by cultural catchphrases. The retreatants wear badges calling them "BACK TO BASICS," but the values espoused at the retreat bear little relation to the air, water, and soil of Kentucky Lake. Business meetings and televised tapes set the decorum for spiritual renewal. Spontaneity yields to program, and feeling submits to ideology. Activity means workshops. The church, in short, brings the city to the country. Shelby wears a clean suit and hastens from session to session gleaning notes on a yellow pad that tabulates "fifty ideas for new sermons" (142). One would expect Scripture to provide Christians with vital topics for preaching; but instead of approaching life through the Book, the church substitutes books for life. Organized groups establish a community in the mind to offset the isolation everyone feels in the heart.

The peril of such a substitution arises at a group discussing Christian marriage, which Georgeann attends. The underlying assumption here is that life abstracted relieves the terror of life lived. The woman conducting the workshop reduces marriage to seven categories of intimacy through which the women share hints for "marriage enhancements" (143). Soon, cerebration usurps sexuality. A fat woman speaks for the debasement of both sexes that such scorn for flesh engenders: "God made man so that he can't resist a woman's adoration. She should treat him as a priceless treasure, for man is the highest form of creation." This dewy-eyed talk goes unchallenged until a tall woman complains that phoniness so fills the world that we are led to "think that the First Lady doesn't have smelly feet" (143). She speaks for Mason. As religion in "The Retreat" encourages an apostasy of the physical, Mason puts in a word for smelly feet and itchy skin. The story argues, moreover, that in an age that dissociates spirit from matter, the body holds open the unknown, the stuff of mystery.

Just how our century can take the mystery out of the body comes to us on the last evening of the retreat, when Georgeann tries to conquer her free-floating sadness. She removes her badge and plays the electronic video games that earlier she saw excited a boy playing them. The machine enthralls her too. Attacking multicolored aliens on the screen liberates Georgeann by giving her momentary control over definite adversaries. The thrill of self-possession also disposes her to the handsome trucker who offers to buy her a beer. Georgeann is hardly a pickup; still, sexual attention reassures her of a physical attractiveness ignored by Shelby. Nothing comes of the encounter. Chasing aliens on the screen blocks all desire in her except for release from a tightening stranglehold. By the time Shelby finds Georgeann, she is depleted by the games. Given the force of her feeling to act decisively, it comes as a surprise that she perceives herself to be a weakling, one of the old invalids requiring Shelby's pastoral cheer. She is not made helpless by age or physical frailty but by infirmity of consciousness, guidance, and resolve resulting from the paralyzing synthetic amusements enchanting her. For Georgeann to fit her spiritual conflicts on a tiny screen shows the compression of which she is capable. Mechanical displacement, however, depersonalizes Georgeann by splitting her body from her mind. Video games blot out "everything but who you are," she tells Shelby with a euphoria discredited by her confusion. What she becomes is a spook. "Your mind leaves your body" (146). Because electronic self-possession is insubstantial, it creates a despairing aloneness.

When the Picketts return to their small brick home, they find a letter reassigning Shelby to a church sixty miles away. Although the house imprisons and change suits her desire for new life, Georgeann refuses to move, "I'm not going with you" (146). The declaration shocks Shelby, and he pulls away from Georgeann's strength and independence. Disdain is his first defense, making her the child before his authority. "What got into you lately, girl?" Before declared pain, his as well as hers, Shelby can only propose evasion. "We can go to a counselor." Shelby does not know how to stand by Georgeann. She realizes that he will write a sermon on the subject for her benefit when he says, "We're going to have to pray over this" (147). His habit of giving abstract value to personal issues drives Shelby to seek solution in the order of reality where it is absent.

Clinging to roles that oppress them conveys the humanness of Mason's characters. Georgeann simultaneously states her intention to be alone and relies on domestic routine to be herself. Before picking up the children, she inspects the chickens. The sick hen still lives and still disturbs her. First, Georgeann takes the eggs to the kitchen; then she gets an ax and decapitates the sick hen. Killing the hen is what Shelby would do to prevent the spread of disease. The precaution is required. Without pausing to reflect, she acts; and in the end she feels that "she has done her duty." These, the last words of "The Retreat," indicate not that Georgeann has cottoned to rules coming "out of nowhere," but that the pressure of organic existence forces certain action. There is the inexplicable confinement she feels at home that compels her to strike out for freedom at the lake and then to pull back once home, and there is the love between her and Shelby that exists without understanding, a love they must live out. Mystery arises in the confluence of physical urgency and the bafflement it stirs. Not the least puzzling quality of this mystery is the way in which the need to be free brings self-restriction.

This paradox takes reverse form in "Third Monday," which brings *Shiloh and Other Stories* to a close by showing that an awareness of limits brings freedom. The story takes up Ruby Jane MacPherson's life between dates at the fairgrounds on the third Monday of each month when she meets her lover Buddy Landon, a dealer along the flea-market circuit. During this interval the Third Monday world of love collapses, and a concealed bond with others quietly emerges. The pattern is set in the opening scene in which the bowling team of Garrison Life Insurance gives a shower for Linda's unborn daughter, Holly, and showers Ruby with reassurance after her radical mastectomy. If our century takes "all the mysteries out of life," as Ruby observes to Linda, then the sympathy of the women puts some promise of surprise back into their lives. With one another the women can be vulnerable and strong in ways that endanger or embarrass them among men. Each has a secret related to the condition Ruby's mother calls "female trouble" (243) that all are trained to hide from males—a miscarriage, severe cramps, and adverse effects of birth control pills. In sharing them, the women lighten the common plight of solitary pain.

Ruby's trouble is the most acute. In the recovery room, she awakes from a nightmare, thinking the pain in her chest comes from a large bird with a hooked beak feeding at her breast. A phantom nurse suckles a feathered monster. "The mound of bandages mystified her" (237). The dread continues into the day. Torn and patched, deprived of her body's mysterious wholeness, bewildered by the need to surrender control of her body to impersonal forces, Ruby must endure the pain of anticipating rejection by the man she loves. A magazine article instills self-loathing with its warning that "he will be disgusted and treat her as though she had been raped, his property violated" (233). Waiting for the results of post-operative tests expands Ruby's terror. Will she be "baptized in a vat of chemicals" (244) like a dog dunked in flea dip? Will they radiate her? Even if her cancer can be treated, there may be no help for the ultimate isolation it imposes. Will Buddy still want to take her home to Tennessee?

By coping with these obscurities, Ruby gains certain recognitions. With Norma Jean, Leroy, and Georgeann, Ruby in physical pain learns that her body has a life of its own. She cannot will her body to be free of malignancy or will it back as it was. For years, she has wisely refused to measure her unmarried independence against conventional images of being a full woman, and now a new wisdom born of loss tells Ruby that she cannot compare her body's shape with magazine versions of a woman's body. Her body after surgery has its own wholeness, demanding a respect for the force of life in it as it is. Breast cancer naturally makes Ruby approach Buddy and the future with doubts and a sense of limits. At the same time, acceptance of limits marks the beginning of overcoming both surgery and apprehension.

The virtue of Ruby's openness becomes clearer when contrasted with Buddy's approach to trouble. His hurt comes from loneliness and the feeble ego defenses used to alleviate pain. He seeks intimacy with Ruby at the same time he fears the vulnerability of being known. Where love would bring closeness, seduction guarantees distance; and so Buddy takes the stance of footloose charmer. Withdrawal protects him, as it does Leroy Moffitt; and the idealized form of a simple dwelling made by their own hands will shelter them. Since Buddy's fear of intimacy is acute, his detachment is extreme. He wants nothing, neither dog nor woman, neither his previous wives nor his present lover. "I don't want anything to remind me of *any*thing" (242), he says while lying next to Ruby in the dark of a motel room. Buddy's physique and good looks are instruments of pride. The cocky swagger he uses to mask his fear of women also endears him to Ruby, who finds freedom in his distance. At the first Third Monday, she hears the far-off yelp of Buddy's beagles and calls his attention to his dogs' crying. "They love me," he responds. "Stick around and you'll love me too" (235).

Ruby does stick around, and does come to love Buddy. The relationship makes her feel less an oddball as a single woman and more a part of the mainstream. Buddy's pickup truck in her driveway pleases Ruby as a display of a man in her life. Despite this nod to conventionality, Ruby is no credulous sentimentalist looking for a romantic lead. Experience with local "ignorant" (237) men who do not accept her as the woman she is forces Ruby to confront her restricted chance for love long before cancer interrupts her life. Wariness over the years disposes her to self-understanding. When, at a bowling match, Betty Lewis advises Ruby to stand firm the moment Buddy learns of her mastectomy and to insist that he love her for herself, Ruby says, "But people always love each other for the wrong reason!" (244). Need is reason enough. In searching for love that does not compromise her integrity, Ruby learns that we live imperfectly and love imperfectly. However circumscribed and irrational, love bridges the gap between Buddy and her and joins Ruby to the world. Third Monday has the unaccountable effect of fulfilling her need to feel, and to feel with others. Ruby welcomes its mystery.

This power to transform is awesome and for Ruby arises from the source at which she experiences deprivation—her body. The entire volume of stories resonates to this motif. "Shiloh" opens the collection with Norma Jean lifting three-pound dumbbells, and near the end of "Third Monday" Ruby raises her right arm to restore vitality to the muscles cut by breast surgery. Mason gives a strong emotional quality to this repeated movement. In strengthening the heroines' bodies, the activity makes them alive again after feeling caught. The prospect of reaching "higher and higher" elates Ruby, "as though there were something tangible above her to reach for" (242). There is something. Stretching her arms mobilizes Ruby for the future. Erect and nonsubmissive, her raised arms point upward to the unknown source of energy.

The last two scenes of "Third Monday" show that there is always the need to reach beyond confinement and that the exigency is felt by everyone. Still weak from surgery, Ruby goes to the fairgrounds on Third Monday to meet Buddy, who is absent. But Gladys, the old black woman who befriended the couple, is there. Too shy to ask Gladys directly about Buddy, Ruby asks about the mushmelon seeds that Gladys boasts have been in her family over a hundred years. "Is that all the way back to slave times?" (245). "Honey," Gladys laughs, "we's in slave times, if you ask me. Slave times ain't never gone out of style, if you know what I mean" (246). Ruby feels what Gladys means upon hearing that Buddy was put in jail in Missouri for selling a stolen television. The story's ending dramatizes the captivity that is our human finitude as Ruby sits in the clinic waiting room, anticipating her checkup. Claustrophobic fear of aggressive therapy stirs in Ruby a panic over being immersed in a vat of chemicals. Her daymare enlarges to imagine Buddy thrashing around a hard bunk in jail. But because immurement jars with Ruby's image of a fancy-free Buddy, she envisions different scenes in which he returns and they depart for the Rockies, a cinematic finale deepened by Ruby's acknowledgment of its improbability. Romantic or indulgent, reaching for intimacy and freedom sustains the heroine. She, a person with cancer, forges an attitude of waiting with hope, not knowing what it is and, more profoundly, not wanting to know what she waits for.

Mason recommends Ruby's humorous imagination by shifting focus at the end to a chubby man sitting next to Ruby in the clinic. The man stops humming to grin as he announces out of the blue that the joyous little girl across the room is his baby. The woman caring for the man explains to Ruby that he loves children and is waiting for his annual brain test. After an unintelligible mutter, he hugs a magazine, another of his babies, and rocks his offspring in his arms. In the end, Ruby has moved from one astonishment to another. She begins the story celebrating Linda's unborn girl and ends watching the man cradling his invented young in his arms. "Third Monday" concludes Ruby's venture and the book by describing the man: "His broad smile curves like the crescent phase of the moon."

The various adventurers into the unknown peopling *Shiloh and Other Stories* unite in the mentally impaired man. Through him Mason suggests that mystery is found in human weakness, precisely in the pitiable helplessness of human life. That the pudgy man's playful grin before life's certain ridiculousness resembles a crescent moon expresses Mason's meaning. The moon presides over formation and breakdown. Change attends its periodic phases so that the moon has no fixed identity. Waxing or waning, crescent beams the becoming of new life—the baby held in the afflicted man's arms and the new life to come with Holly's birth. The same current operates in the lunar pattern of Ruby Jane MacPherson's story. Between monthly meetings with Buddy, Ruby's body suffers change, but crisis propels her toward the expectant unknown. Bobbie Ann Mason leaves Ruby and the other protagonists in transition from entrapment to a new reaching out for release from the slave quarters of isolation and infirmity. A secret attraction persists at a hidden level of their psyche to the unknown and the new personal form. Mystery implies creativity. Despite every contrary experience, Mason's characters look for change and freedom at the heart of reality. The essence of their life in western Kentucky is not its geographical remoteness or cultural strictures but its interior discoveries of the mystery that their lives add up to something beyond themselves.

Note

1. Mason acknowledges rural Southernness as the condition shaping her characters and their action (Wilhelm), but she is simultaneously aware of approaching the South in a way that subordinates its tradition to the urgencies of the present. Her Southerners do not struggle to preserve the bygone order that would alienate them from the hum and buzz of modern life. Transformation and growth, not estrangement and retrenchment, engage their imagination. "I think where I wind up now is writing about people who are trying to get into the mainstream," Mason says, "or they're in the mainstream, just trying to live their lives the best they can" (Rothstein 50). Mason, unlike Walker Percy, does not regard the modern world as a desert of arid ruin or the Babylon of earthly abominations or the radioactive field on which the last days are playing themselves out in acid rain. Sam Hughes, the young heroine of Mason's first novel, *In Country* (1985), handles the grief over the death of her father in Vietnam (killed before she was born) by sympathizing with the terrible effects of the war as she

travels from western Kentucky to the Vietnam Memorial in Washington.

Readers have been more guardedly enthusiastic about *Spence + Lila* (1988), which tells of a farm family, first scattered by the cultural movements of its children, then reunited when the mother, Lila Culpepper, has breast cancer. Reviewers express disappointment in finding only the skill they expect of Mason and judge *Spence + Lila* to be more a poignant (Kakutani 18) and occasionally "brilliant" (Conroy) confirmation of Mason's established technique. Familiar now with her deliberate restrictions of style and subject, commentators call Mason a minimalist and group her with Raymond Carver, Frederick Barthelme, and Mary Robison, other chroniclers of working-class America (Rothstein 96).

Works Cited

Barnes, Linda Adams. "The Freak Endures: The Southern Grotesque from Flannery O'Connor to Bobbie Ann Mason." *Since Flannery O'Connor: Essays in the Contemporary American Short Story.* Ed. Loren Logsdon and Charles W. Mayer, Macomb: Western Illinois UP, 1987, 133–41.

Brinkmeyer, Robert H., Jr. "Finding One's History: Bobbie Ann Mason and Contemporary Southern Literature." *The Southern Literary Journal* 19 (1987): 20–33.

Conroy, Frank. "The Family at Her Bedside." Rev. of *Spence + Lila*, by Bobbie Ann Mason. *New York Times Book Review* 26 June 1988: 7.

Kakutani, Michiko. "Struggle and Hope in the New South." Rev. of *Spence + Lila*, by Bobbie Ann Mason. *New York Times* 11 June 1988, late ed.: 18.

Mason, Bobbie Ann. *In Country.* New York: Harper, 1985.

———. *Shiloh and Other Stories.* 1982. New York: Perennial-Harper, 1985.

———. *Spence + Lila.* Illustrations by LaNella Mason. New York: Harper, 1988.

Rothstein, Mervyn. "Homegrown Fiction: Bobbie Ann Mason Blends Springsteen and Nabokov." *New York Times Magazine* 15 May 1988: 50, 98–9, 101, 108.

Wilhelm, Albert E. "An Interview with Bobbie Ann Mason." *The Southern Quarterly* 26 (1988): 27–38.

Leslie White

When the action in a story or novel approaches camp or sentimentality then skirts it so deftly that the shock, the pathos, the comedy, the affirmation or whatever mood might come to characterize a given scene becomes authentic, that fiction takes power from the risk, the risk of destruction by parody. This kind of scene works partly because the reader is put off balance, and doesn't know if he likes what he has read because of the action itself or because of the risk that the writer has taken, or just happened upon. Whether they are or not, the artist's intent and the fiction appear seamless. The final episode of Bobbie Ann Mason's *In Country* is such a scene. Mason lets the fictional context generate every cliche possible, and parody is neutralized by sheer accumulation of cliche.

Seventeen-year-old Samantha (Sam) Hughes is the novel's protagonist; in "the summer of the Michael Jackson *Victory* tour and the Bruce Springsteen *Born in the U.S.A.* tour" (23), Sam has become obsessed with the war that killed her father before she was born, and in this final scene she has come to the Vietnam Memorial with her uncle Emmett, himself a veteran who may have been exposed to agent orange, and her "Mamaw" Hughes. When they locate Dwayne Hughes's name on panel 9E and find it is out of Sam and Mamaw's reach, two workmen lend their ladder and Emmett holds it as the magnificently obese Mamaw— crying, mumbling as she climbs, terrified that someone will look up her dress—stretches to finger the inscription. Mason goes for humor here, and this is a funny moment, very nearly cartoonish, but finally affecting. Impressive as Mason's handling of this potentially preposterous situation is, what is most interesting and thematically significant here is Sam's moving up the ladder clutching a just-purchased copy of Bruce Springsteen's album *Born in the U.S.A.* In a novel so full of references to popular culture, especially pop music, we might read this detail as mere

"The Function of Popular Culture in Bobbie Ann Mason's *Shiloh and Other Stories* and *In Country*," from *Southern Quarterly* 26 (Summer 1988): 69–79. © 1988 by the University of Southern Mississippi. Reprinted by permission.

representation of that culture, which is to say, not notice it at all. Mason wants this reaction probably, for Sam's carrying the Springsteen album up the ladder is itself unconscious action; in a split second it gets internalized. As part of Sam's everyday experience, it is no more significant than opening a can of Pepsi and no less than validating her father's existence by touching the carved letters of his name.

Fictionists, poets and playwrights of the last thirty years have had to be willing to confront elements of popular culture. Many have been curious to know if a piece of popular art is worth anything culturally and aesthetically, and if it can live up to the life it enters. Usually, of course, it can't. One takes it in and it most often fragments, or disappears, or worse, humiliates the intimate moment of acceptance and enthusiasm. Working elements of popular culture into a story, poem or play merely allows a certain kind of realism; a song, a movie, a video, a soap or rock star can precisely nail a narrative in time and place. A vital piece of popular culture may favorably shape one's view of the world, enable him to become more engaged in life, allow him to read and respond to the images of his world with greater precision. At its worst, pop culture wipes out the immediate reality by occupying the space where real engagement might take place. Mason's grainy portraits of small-town America, written in a deadpan prose, are an appropriate *mise-en-scene* for examining the interplay between people and popular culture, and this is where Mason works, though she appears to eschew any profound meaning in popular art.

> I think it's [popular culture] very close to people and it reflects what they feel and believe. Certain people denigrate it because it's not high art, but I don't happen to feel that way. I don't want to have an elitist attitude about the culture. It's very real, it means something to a whole lot of people, and I can't ignore that. . . . I'm not so interested in what it means ultimately—whether *M*A*S*H** is a good show or not . . . whether we're being manipulated by these images. I'm just after the quality of experience in everyday life. Things like that have significance. (Smith 425)

For Mason, part of what makes up "the quality of experience in everyday life"—at least in her fiction—is not only the generic furniture of mass culture but the "significance" of popular art ("what it means ultimately") as well. In other words, no matter how banal, demeaning or forgettable, popular culture is formative, and in Mason's fiction it appears as the foreground on which her characters move. Mason's treatment of popular culture—and popular music in particular—in *Shiloh and Other Stories* and *In Country* provokes aggressive questions about that culture, its effect on us and about the nature of art in a high technology society; how does pop culture enter into the lives of people and what is its function there? If people even bother to take it in, or if they unknowingly absorb it, what then do they do with it? How good or schlocky does a piece of pop culture have to be in order to make it into fiction? Is pop culture less significant when it is just part of the day-to-day than when it bears hard on the day-to-day?

The desolate stories of *Shiloh* surrender the hallowed southern sense of place to a deadly blanketing of popular culture. Mason's company of seemingly interchangeable characters amounts to a collective image that isolates a crucial paradox of American life, born of the shaky belief that America is "blessed, [and] the lingering suspicion that it is cursed" (Marcus 60). Mason locates her characters' places along this continuum in speaking of "Residents and Transients," a story she considers "the focal point for the main theme in *Shiloh*":

> I don't think the people I write about are obsessed with the past. I don't think they know anything about the Civil War, and I don't think they care. They're kind of naive and optimistic for the most part: they think better times are coming, and most of them embrace progress. But I think they reflect that tension that's in the culture between hanging onto the past and racing toward the future. . . . [T]here are some people who would just never leave home, because that's where they're meant to be; and others, are, well, born to run. (Smith 425)

This subject of rootlessness at once puts Mason squarely in the southern tradition of expatriation by justifying the value of place and points up the inefficacy of region nowadays to provide identity. To get her version of rural America where regional demarcations no longer exist, Mason ransacks the South of her parents and grandparents and draws characters who are stuck in the remembered life of some idealized South or who forsake their region in pursuit of whatever it is they think "home" can't provide. On a familiar enough southern landscape, Mason throws the Kmart culture of pray TV, video games and videos, *Wheel of Fortune, Phil Donahue*, subdivisions and trailer parks and bad pop music. The result may be a literature of the New South, a kind of white trash chic, but it reads more like the destruction of white trash.

Pink flamingos, wagon wheels and shelling peas on the front porch give way to crocheted Star Trek pillow covers, electric garage doors and learning how to write English compositions. In the collection's title story, Norma Jean Moffitt transforms Donovan's "Sunshine Superman" into a latinized Holiday Inn number on her multifunctioned organ, then remarks: "I didn't like these old songs back then. But I have this crazy feeling I missed something" (3). Norma Jean's husband, Leroy, sensing, her restlessness, tells her that she "didn't miss a thing" (3). Like Norma Jean, Mack ("The Rookers") feels "he has missed something" (21), but rather than reacting against what he knows is attention to the mere form of life, he ices over. He becomes "absorbed in something on TV, a pudding commercial" (20), reads bestsellers and Carl Sagan's *Cosmos* but "does not believe anything he has read" because it "was not on TV in their part of the country" (24). After hearing the Oak Ridge Boys singing "Elvira" on the radio, Dolores ("The Climber") notes that they "used to be a gospel quartet when [she] was a child. Now, inexplicably, they are a group of young men with blow dried hair, singing country-rock songs about love" (115). These are familiar people in Mason's fiction. Though removed from the mainstream, they are nevertheless affected by its trends and policies and tempted by its images of affluence and prosperity. Complacent but restless, inarticulate about their frustrations, they are grotesques in a way, products of a culture that asks nothing of them and rewards their compliance.

One could say that these failures are merely failures of nerve, or perhaps that they even further bear out a caveat of the fugitives, who sixty years ago feared the annihilation of regional integrity, cultural uniqueness and the centrality of community by industrial advance. Whatever these details signify, this fiction is *fin-de-siecle* stuff, and barely recognizable as a literature of the South. As fiction that tries to escape both form and region, while acknowledging it wouldn't exist without them, it is a literature of rural America strained away from history and tradition. Its men and women are adrift from any meaningful regional identification and have become dazed objects of a mass culture that is too accessible, that is by nature amoral and that throws the emotions, values and ideas of the populace back on itself. At its worst, this culture tends to reduce, to contain the lives that come across it, though when it works as the pure democratic expression it is, it liberates and provides a way of sharing something special with others. Behind the exhilaration of such a mass collective response is a chief irony of the pop process, which Mason addresses in both *Shiloh* and *In Country;* how can a movie, a song, a TV star, a politician, anyone or anything that moves beyond cult status retain specialness, the ability to provoke, disturb, entertain?

155

Part 3

Mason participates in the tradition of American art which seeks to destroy the culture's romanticized image of itself, and her fictionalizing of the country's single, original cultural expression allows a tough look at the workings of democracy. The *Shiloh* stories are about the maintenance of cultural homogeneity, about what can happen when people fail to prevent aspects of their culture from trivializing life, drying it up, turning it bland and narrow. Mason writes also to find out what brand of popular art destroys naivete, which kinds are threatening, which are powerful or seductive enough in themselves to demean a life, or enrich it.

A number of the men and women in the *Shiloh* stories are survivors of a powerful counterculture that burned out before it could establish itself politically and philosophically. Though none of them—except perhaps Nancy Culpepper and her husband Jack ("Nancy Culpepper") or Mary ("Residents and Transients")—ever held a building or discussed Dylan's poetics, they all long nostalgically for some cultural anchor, one they seem to have known only vaguely or feel they missed altogether. In exploring the surface cleared by the counterculture, Mason comes up with a literature of the '60s, an odd admixture of '70s retreat into psychobabble, '80s capitulation, the commercializing of what was once important and sustaining to youthful communities, and the standardizing of emotions and privileges. When Mason uses popular culture in her stories and particularly when she reveals her people through the music that they either ignored, reveled in or listened to out of obligation, her stories open up to show characters asking tough questions, wondering about the consequences of risk, reacting against past decisions made out of lust for thoughtless security, or out of ignorance.

"A New-Wave Format" is such a story, with such a central character, and thus is atypical of the collection's depiction of popular culture as a pervasive stupefying presence. The story's protagonist is Edwin Creech, a bus driver who transports mentally retarded adults to training classes at the Cedar Hill Mental Health Center. At forty-three, twice divorced and in love with twenty-year-old Sabrina, Edwin, like many another character in *Shiloh*, desperately tries to order his world by sorting through what now seems to him a staggeringly uneventful past. Edwin believes "he has gone through life rather blindly, without much pain or sense of loss" (216), as if "pain and loss" could destroy his love of control—really a self-love—that has retarded mobility and smothered curiosity.

On the bus, a new luxury model with a tape deck, AM-FM, CB, and built in first-aid kit, Edwin plays tape recorded music to "calm and

156

entertain the passengers," to "keep his distance and keep order at the same time" (217).

> In effect, he has become a disc jockey, taking requests and using the microphone, but he avoids fast talk. The supervisors at the center have told him that the developmentally disabled—they always use this term—need a world that is slowed down; they can't keep up with today's fast pace. So he plays mellow old sixties tunes by the Lovin' Spoonful, Joni Mitchell, Donovan. It seems to work, (217).

In Edwin's mind, Sabrina's preoccupation with her bit part in *Oklahoma!* turns her every action to performance; in response to her histrionics, which he can't separate from the "sappy *Oklahoma!* sound" (221), Edwin "finds himself playing a few Dylan tunes, some Janis Joplin, nothing too hectic." This is "music he did not understand fifteen years ago, music that now seems full of possibility: the Grateful Dead, the Jefferson Airplane, groups with vision" (222). Admitting that his whole life has been a "delayed reaction," Edwin begins to seek something authentic and immediate, but he seeks it through conscious attachment rather than through intuitive response. That he hasn't taken this well-intentioned self-examination far enough, has in fact just begun it, becomes clear when "a stringbean girl" gives him a Plasmatics tape and he snaps, "I don't play new-wave. I have a golden-oldie format. I just play sixties stuff" (222). Edwin's adherence to safe programming betrays a counterfeit life of disengagement and prescription. Like Sabrina, who believes that fulfillment originates outside the self, Edwin justifies his passivity by noting "that he has bypassed some critical stage in his life: a knowledge of terror" (217), and thinks that one look at this "terror" will instantly renovate twenty years of aimlessness and surrender. Edwin's steady move toward greater self-knowledge—the real "knowledge of terror"—is intuitive in origin and essential nature (as such movements tend to be), though he tries to explain any insight and its palpable consequences as rational and inevitable, as if to do what is in accord with one's deepest self is a linear, schematic progression.

Abruptly, following Sabrina's advice, Edwin shifts formats. Because of his fear that the music will result in chaos on the bus, Edwin offers a Doors revival as "a bridge from the past to the present, spanning those empty years—his marriages, the turbulence of the times—and connecting his youth solidly with the present" (228). Later, when he works in "Squeeze, the B-52s, the Psychedelic Furs, the Flying Lizards, Frankie and the Knockouts," Edwin sees that "the passengers understood what was happening. The frantic beat was a perfect expression of their aimlessness and frustration" (228), and a perfect disruption of his. When one of the passengers has a seizure, Edwin reacts quickly with first-aid measures and gets the man to a hospital. His supervisors commend him for his quick action, call him a hero, but the trip to the hospital amid his passengers' "screams, long and drawn out . . . eerie and supernatural" (229) leaves Edwin shaken; he steadies himself with a Donovan cassette, puts himself back on familiar ground. This is a kind of retreat, only natural after a hard stare at something real, but Edwin has gotten his glimpse of terror, and it is enough for now. Edwin's movement from "mellow sixties tunes" to a new-wave format might indicate some kind of progression in musical taste, and it may be too much to say that this movement has caused a transformation of personality or that it reflects increasing self-awareness. Clearly, though, it is the subversive element in the music that he knows—from Dylan's witty irreverence and Lennon's weary anger to a fagged out punk rant—that gets him as close to his "knowledge of terror" as he is likely to come. It sends Edwin inside for a look at the real source of his failures, and he comes to the uneasy realization that the meaning and worth of whatever one is comfortable with too often issue from the fear of its opposite. While this conclusion is especially grim, Edwin's experience nevertheless suggests that he has found out how to surrender to something vital outside himself—in this case music, a medium that had always been there to comment on his life, even alter it.

In a culture leveled to homogeneity by the diffusive, seductive tendencies of democracy, Mason's characters look for something moving across the surface of life that can give them sustenance, that can comment on their lives in such a way that they may have a chance to feel at home, and find out who they are. In the stories of *Shiloh*, popular culture is most often a barrage of brand names, media stars and sales pitches that obscures with a soft and sinister blatancy the relationships between people and whatever might interest them; so, very little connects. With *In Country*, however, though Mason continues to see popular culture as impairing one's ability to distinguish between what is fake and what isn't, she mainly explores its potential to tighten the breach between cultural images and individual perceptions. Mason's fictional world, then, noticeably transforms from a kind of anti-terrain where popular culture merely betrays what it helped create (or where it is dysfunctional altogether, just junk on the periphery) to a riskier, more resonant terrain where it can stick, where it can mean something for those who are willing to do something with the best and worst of it.

In Country begins with its epigraph, these lines from Bruce Springsteen's four minute image of betrayal, "Born in the U.S.A."; "I'm ten years burning down the road / Nowhere to run ain't got nowhere to go." The song tells the story of a Vietnam veteran denied re-entry into the society he went off to defend. Its sound and concept are massive, its imagery as stark as anything in *Going After Cacciato* or *Apocalypse Now*. What the epigraph itself dramatizes is a flight and displacement that turn Springsteen's familiar romanticism of the open road into ugly culde-sac. And its mood of fury and desperation powerfully surrounds the novel so that throughout, the story struggles to live up to the image, mirror it, or escape its uneasy mixture of horror, relief and resignation. Rather than issuing naturally from the epigraph, the novel chases it.

In Country's originality is its dramatization of Vietnam's legacy through the experience of someone who gets her account secondhand.

> It was the summer of the Michael Jackson *Victory* tour and the Bruce Springsteen *Born in the U.S.A.* tour, neither of which Sam got to go to. At her graduation, the commencement speaker, a Methodist minister, had preached about keeping the country strong, stressing sacrifice. He made Sam nervous. She started thinking about war, and it stayed on her mind all summer. (23)

About all Sam Hughes knows about Vietnam is that "Emmett came back . . . but [her] father did not" (23). These words read like plain fact, but to Sam they take on the character of a riddle. That her father didn't come back *is* a fact, and Sam's recognition that Emmett and many another didn't either and her acceptance of the America that Vietnam made drive the novel. Part of what makes solving the riddle so difficult is Sam's dogged reaching after facts and reasons, an insistence most often met with evasiveness and apathy. Even her mother tells her, "Don't fret too much over this Vietnam thing, Sam. You shouldn't feel bad about any of it. It had nothing to do with you" (57). Sam knows this is a lie and eventually accepts that she can't understand the real reasons for the war's prolongation. But she can see its effects all around her—the way it stunts, the way it keeps men from growing up, the way it makes men "nostalgic about killing" (209). But before she learns these things, the riddle of "coming home" becomes for Sam a curse, and she will not get out from under its weight until she stares at the inscription of her father's name and takes the curse itself as bare fact.

159

Part 3

Playing in Sam's mind continuously is the music that she knows so well, the music that ties her to her mother (now remarried, with a new baby and living in Louisville), to Emmett, and to the war years. At a dance for Hopewell's veterans, one vet comments, "When you're in country, there's so little connection to the World, but those songs—that was as close as we came to a real connection" (111). Here is the first clue to the riddle, for it allows Sam to break through the barrier of amnesia and paralysis that closes off the world of *In Country*. From here

> Sam tried to imagine Grace Slick bellowing ["White Rabbit"] out at the enemy. With that kind of music, why didn't the North Vietnamese just lay down their weapons and get stoned? If they had understood English, maybe the music would have won the war. But now, listening to "All You Need Is Love," she realized how naive the words were. Love didn't even solve things for two people, much less the whole world, she thought. But it wasn't only the words. Sometimes the music was full of energy and hope and the words were just the opposite. Emmett had said rock-and-roll was happy music about sad stuff. (111)

Rock 'n' roll and the feeling of being "in country" seem inseparable to Sam, and the spirit and promise of the music convince her that as close as she can come to the Vietnam experience is to create a version of it out by swampy Cawood's Pond, a place "so dangerous even the Boy Scouts wouldn't camp out there" (208). She becomes completely caught up in the night, smelling banana leaves, the "special gook stink" that her father had written of in his journal, and she imagines wading through rice paddies "with snakes winding themselves around her legs" (212). When she hears what she thinks are footsteps, she imagines a VC, then fears a rapist and finally, just for a moment, a "curious pleasure stole over her. This terror was what the soldiers had felt every minute" (217). This terror is what she's after, but it is evanescent: "In a few moments, everything would be clear and fine" (218).

The footsteps turn out to be real; they are Emmett's and in the dawn at Cawood's Pond, after hearing Sam's story, Emmett appears ready to open up about his inability to fit back in, his unwillingness to absorb the experience. Waiting for a revelation, something definitive, Sam is shocked by the pathetic ordinariness of Emmett's admission, as though what he tells her is not explanation enough for his problems: "This is what I *do*. I work on staying together, one day at a time. There's no room for anything else" (225). Emmett's burden is the contradiction that he understands fully, or at least better than the other vets in the novel:

confronting his Vietnam experience in some way is essential if he is to cope with it, yet it has become a self-consciousness that needs to be exorcised. Before he can achieve the kind of anti-self-consciousness necessary for participation in the human community, or for his return to it, Emmett must somehow surrender to the kind of abandon and resignation expressed in "Born in the U.S.A." As the vet in the song has done, Emmett needs to let "I'm ten years burning down the road" become "I'm a long gone daddy in the U.S.A." Or better, he needs to hold both in mind at once.

Emmett's challenge is to recreate the self by becoming oblivious to it, and to accept the hard facts of the past as events that happened. He tells Sam, "You can't learn from the past. The main thing you learn from history is that you can't learn from history. That's what history *is*" (226). Sam's furious reaching after the facts of the war years is both salutary and futile and she accepts more than internalizes the notion that history can show us nothing but the events of a particular time and place. The only real connection to the past for Sam is the music, the sixties rock 'n' roll tradition as handed down to contemporary figures like Springsteen. The past is accessible to Sam through sensations, then, not through facts and theories of war and culture. The real connection to her father, to the war, and to the counterculture is the popular music that evokes the mood of the period. Music transcends historical fact, while the facts of history obscure the absolute, handing us a version of the past wanting mythic resonance. And for Sam, who longs for the energy of the sixties, the music is an essential nostalgia.

Mason has recently referred to her " 'writing as my version of rock 'n' roll. . . .' Both are 'a kind of positive energy' that embody . . . 'hope for a better world' " ("Writer's Desk" 80). Because Mason writes fiction and not rock songs, in hoping for a better world she looks first to find out what can make life limiting and unfulfilling. Across the neon and billboard rural landscape move men and women—numbed by their own limited intentions—whose acquiescence illustrates a persistent American irony: the promise of utopia and success set against the fact of separation and failure. Mason depicts this irony variously, but perhaps most sharply by examining how popular culture affects lived experience. The best popular culture has always justified itself by disturbing the peace on the one hand and on the other by commenting on the reality most said it blurred if not denied altogether. The worst popular art creations, and perhaps the most destructive, are "designed not to trouble, but to reassure; they do not reflect reality, they merely rearrange its elements into something we can bear" (Baldwin 31). Mass culture of this sort is flimsy, escapist, superficial, but often as dangerous, as manipulative and as interesting as the most provocative "high art." Baldwin comments that popular culture "can only reflect our chaos: and perhaps we better remember that this chaos contains life—and a great transforming energy" (32). In *Shiloh*, popular culture most often functions divisively, isolating the characters or tranquilizing them; but in her novel, Mason shows how popular art, especially popular music, can be a means of continuity and communication. Mason wouldn't disagree that popular culture reflects our chaos, but she seems more drawn to those elements and kinds of popular art which create it (producing a vital spark in the culture) and those which destroy it (creating a cultural exhaustion that just might lead to growth through decay) but mostly to what happens to people as these impulses vie for ascendence.

Works Cited

Baldwin, James. "Mass Culture and the Creative Artist." *The Popular Arts in America: A Reader.* Ed. William M. Hammel. New York: Harcourt. 1972. 29–32.

Marcus, Greil. *Mystery Train: Images of America in Rock 'n' Roll Music.* New York: Dutton. 1975.

Mason, Bobbie Ann. *In Country.* New York: Harper, 1985.

———. *Shiloh and Other Stories.* New York: Harper, 1982.

Smith, Wendy. "*PW* Interviews Bobbie Ann Mason," *Publisher's Weekly* 30 Aug. 1985: 424–25.

"A Writer's Desk." *Saturday Review* Nov./Dec. 1985: 80.

Chronology

1940	Bobbie Ann Mason born 1 May, to Wilburn A. and Christianna Lee Mason in Mayfield, Kentucky.
1954–1958	Attends Mayfield High School.
1954	Becomes national president of Hilltoppers fan club. During next four years attends concerts throughout the Midwest. Writes and edits *Hilltopper Topics*, the fan club newsletter.
1958–1962	Attends the University of Kentucky. Writes columns for school newspaper and publishes fiction in campus literary magazine. Works during summers as writer for *Mayfield Messenger*, Mayfield, Kentucky.
1962	Graduates from the University of Kentucky with B.A. in English. Employed by Ideal Publishing Company, New York City, as a writer for fan magazines.
1963	Leaves New York City to enter graduate school.
1966	Receives M.A. in English from State University of New York at Binghamton. Enters Ph.D. program at the University of Connecticut.
1969	Marries Roger B. Rawlings on 12 April.
1971	Moves with husband to Mansfield, Pennsylvania, where Rawlings teaches English at Mansfield State College.
1972	Receives Ph.D. in English from the University of Connecticut after writing dissertation on Nabokov's *Ada*. Begins teaching part-time at Mansfield State College.
1974	Ardis Press publishes *Nabokov's Garden: A Guide to* Ada.
1975	Feminist Press publishes *The Girl Sleuth*.
1978	Begins submitting short stories to the *New Yorker*.
1979	Publishes "The Elements of E. B. White's Style" in *Language Arts*. Leaves teaching position to write full-time.

1980   18 February issue of the *New Yorker* contains "Offerings," Mason's first published story (except for contribution to student literary magazine); "Shiloh" appears in the 20 October issue. Mason begins writing "Talk of the Town" pieces for the *New Yorker*. Moves with husband to southeast Pennsylvania.

1981   "Shiloh" selected for *Best American Short Stories, 1981*.

1982   Harper & Row publishes *Shiloh and Other Stories*. This collection receives nominations for National Book Critics Circle Award and American Book Award.

1983   *Shiloh and Other Stories* receives Ernest Hemingway Foundation Award and nomination for PEN-Faulkner Award. "Graveyard Day" selected for *Best American Short Stories, 1983* and Pushcart Prize VIII. Mason receives a fellowship from National Endowment for the Arts. A visit to the Vietnam Veterans Memorial in Washington (where she sees on the wall a version of her own name, Bobby G. Mason) inspires the final section of *In Country*.

1984   Receives Guggenheim fellowship and an award from American Academy and Institute for Arts and Letters. Publishes first magazine travel feature, "Jamaica," in April issue of *Esquire*.

1985   Harper & Row publishes *In Country*.

1986   "Big Bertha Stories" selected for *Prize Stories 1986: The O. Henry Awards;* 26 May issue of the *New Yorker* features "Reaching the Stars" (an excerpt from a projected memoir).

1987   Publishes first signed humor piece, "La Bamba Hot Line," in 7 September issue of the *New Yorker*.

1988   Harper & Row publishes *Spence + Lila*; "Bumblebees" selected for *Prize Stories 1988: The O. Henry Awards*.

1989   Harper & Row publishes *Love Life: Stories*. Vietnam Veterans of America honors Mason for her novel *In Country* with its first President's Citation, recognizing a nonveteran who has contributed to public understanding of the war and its consequences. Warner Brothers releases a film version of *In Country* directed by Norman Jewison.

1990   Moves, with husband, back to Kentucky after lengthy residence in Northeast.

1991   Receives Appalachian Medallion Award. "With Jazz" selected for *New Stories from the South: The Year's Best, 1991.*

1993   HarperCollins publishes *Feather Crowns*, which becomes cowinner of the Southern Book Award for fiction and finalist for National Book Critics Circle Award.

1994   Receives honorary doctorate from University of Kentucky and delivers commencement address.

1995   Receives honorary doctorate from Eastern Kentucky University. University of Georgia Press reissues *The Girl Sleuth*. University Press of Kentucky reissues *Shiloh and Other Stories*. 16 October issue of the *New Yorker* publishes "The Chicken Tower," excerpt from a memoir in progress.

1996   Writes introduction to *The American Claimant* for the *Oxford Mark Twain*, Oxford University Press. "Proper Gypsies" selected for Pushcart Prize XXI and cited in *Best American Short Stories, 1996.*

1997   22 December issue of the *New Yorker* publishes "The Burden of the Feast," excerpt from memoir in progress.

1998   Ecco Press publishes *Midnight Magic*, a short story collection consisting of stories from *Shiloh and Other Stories* and *Love Life*, with introduction by the author. Ecco also reissues *Spence + Lila*.

Selected Bibliography

Primary Sources

Individual Stories

"Offerings." *New Yorker,* 18 February 1980, 31–33.
"Fan City." *Redbook,* September 1980, 31+.
"Shiloh." *New Yorker,* 20 October 1980, 50–57.
"Nancy Culpepper." *New Yorker,* 9 February 1981, 34–42.
"Etheleen's Collection." *Epoch* 30 (Spring–Summer 1981): 175–87.
"Rushing." *Delaware Today,* May 1981, 40–45.
"Detroit Skyline, 1949." *Atlantic,* June 1981, 44–46+.
"Old Things." *North American Review,* September 1981, 41–47.
"Recreation." *Bloodroot* (Winter 1981); 11–23. [Revised and retitled "The Ocean"
     in *Shiloh and Other Stories*]
"Drawing Names." *Atlantic,* December 1981, 55–61.
"Still Life with Watermelon." *Redbook,* January 1982, 100–101+.
"Graveyard Day." *Ascent* 7 (1982): 1–12.
"Underground." *Virginia Quarterly Review* 58 (Spring 1982): 291–99.
"The Retreat." *Atlantic,* July 1982, 40–45.
"Third Monday." *New Yorker,* 2 August 1982, 32–40.
"The Climber." *Washington Post Magazine,* 8 August 1982, 20–23.
"Residents and Transients." *Boston Review* 7 (August 1982): 12–15.
"A New-Wave Format." *Atlantic,* November 1982, 62–69.
"Gooseberry Winter." *Redbook,* November 1982, 28+.
"The Rookers." In *Shiloh and Other Stories.* [See below]
"Lying Doggo." In *Shiloh and Other Stories.* [See below]
"Private Lies." *Atlantic,* March 1983, 62–67.
"Harvest." *Bloodroot,* Spring 1983, 5–10.
"New Ground." *North American Review,* June 1983, 30–32.
"Airwaves." *Atlantic,* August 1983, 40–46+.
"Aunt Hatt." *Washington Post Magazine,* 14 August 1983, 8+.
"Hunktown." *Atlantic,* January 1984, 56–64.
"Do You Know What It Means to Miss New Orleans?" *Paris Review* 26 (Fall
     1984): 79–92.
"Love Life." *New Yorker,* 29 October 1984, 42–50.

"Big Bertha Stories." *Mother Jones*, April 1985, 10–12+.

"Murphey's Pond." *Crazyhorse*, Fall 1985, 105–13.

"Blue Country." *Boston Globe Magazine*, 8 September 1985, 20+.

"State Champions." *Harper's*, February 1987, 68–72+.

"Bumblebees." *New Yorker*, 9 March 1987, 32–40.

"Midnight Magic." *New Yorker*, 24 August 1987, 26–33.

"Company." *Boston Globe Magazine*, 27 September 1987, 16+.

"Memphis." *New Yorker*, 22 February 1988, 34–42.

"Marita." *Mother Jones*, May 1988, 41–46.

"The Secret of the Pyramids." *Boston Globe Magazine*, 15 May 1988, 26+.

"Wish." *New Yorker*, 18 May 1988, 28–32.

"Sorghum." *Paris Review* 30 (Summer 1988): 206–21.

"Coyotes." *New Yorker*, 13 June 1988, 29–38.

"Piano Fingers." *Southern Magazine*, November 1988, 46+.

"With Jazz." *New Yorker*, 26 February 1990, 44–50.

"Tobrah." *Story* 38 (Summer 1990): 10–25.

"Weeds." *Boston Globe Magazine*, 25 November 1990, 20–28.

"Rolling into Atlanta." *Ploughshares* 17 (Winter 1991–92): 193–208.

"Shooting the Dog." *Southern Review* 28 (Autumn 1992): 780–89.

"The Afternoon Before the Morning." In *First Words: Earliest Writing from Favorite Contemporary Authors*, edited by Paul Mandelbaum, 346–53. Chapel Hill, N.C.: Algonquin Books, 1993.

"Proper Gypsies." *Southern Review* 31 (Autumn 1995): 833–44.

"Nancy Drew Remembers." In *Murder for Love*, edited by Otto Penzler, 203–28. New York: Delacorte Press, 1996.

"Thunder Snow." *Doubletake* 3 (Spring 1997): 106–10.

"Window Lights." *Story* 45 (Autumn 1997): 51–58.

"Charger." *Atlantic*, January 1998, 66–76.

Short Story Collections

Love Life. New York: Harper & Row, 1989. Includes "Love Life," "Midnight Magic," "Hunktown," "Marita," "The Secret of the Pyramids," "Piano Fingers," "Bumblebees," "Big Bertha Stories," "State Champions," "Private Lies," "Coyotes," "Airwaves," "Sorghum," "Memphis," "Wish."

Midnight Magic. Hopewell, N.J.: Ecco Press, 1998. Stories selected from previous collections with new introduction by author.

Shiloh and Other Stories. New York: Harper & Row, 1982. Includes "Shiloh," "The Rookers," "Detroit Skyline, 1949," "Offerings," "Still Life with Watermelon," "Old Things," "Drawing Names," "The Climber," "Residents and Transients," "The Retreat," "The Ocean," "Graveyard Day," "Nancy Culpepper," "Lying Doggo," "A New-Wave Format," "Third Monday."

Novels

Feather Crowns. New York: HarperCollins, 1993.
In Country. New York: Harper & Row, 1985.
Spence + Lila. New York: Harper & Row, 1988.

Nonfiction Books

The Girl Sleuth: A Feminist Guide to the Bobbsey Twins, Nancy Drew, and Their Sisters.
    Old Westbury, N.Y.: Feminist Press, 1974. Preface to the New Edition by
    Bobbie Ann Mason. Athens: University of Georgia Press, 1995.
Nabokov's Garden: A Guide to Ada. Ann Arbor: Ardis, 1974.

Nonfiction Essays

"Creating Meaning out of the Chaos." *Baltimore Evening Sun,* 12 April 1988, A19.
"The Elements of E. B. White's Style." *Language Arts* 56 (September 1979):
    692–96.
"Nancy Drew: The Once and Future Prom Queen." In *Feminism in Women's Detective Fiction,* edited by Glenwood H. Irons, 74–93. Toronto: University of
    Toronto Press, 1995.
"Reaching the Stars: My Life as a Fifties Groupie." *New Yorker,* 26 May 1986,
    30–38. Reprinted in *A World Unsuspected: Portraits of Southern Childhood,*
    edited by Alex Harris, 53–77. Chapel Hill: University of North Carolina
    Press, 1987.
[Untitled contribution to "A Symposium on Contemporary American Fiction"].
    In *Writers and Their Craft: Short Stories and Essays on the Narrative,* edited by
    Nicholas Delbanco and Laurence Goldstein, 176–77. Detroit, Mich.:
    Wayne State University Press, 1991.
[Untitled introduction to "Shiloh"]. In *American Voices: Best Short Fiction by Contemporary Authors,* edited by Sally Arteseros, 335. New York: Hyperion, 1992.

Secondary Sources

Interviews

Gholson, Craig. "Bobbie Ann Mason." *BOMB* 28 (Summer 1989): 40–43.
Havens, Lila. "Residents and Transients: An Interview with Bobbie Ann
    Mason." *Crazyhorse* 29 (Fall 1985): 87–104.
Hill, Dorothy Combs. "An Interview with Bobbie Ann Mason." *Southern Quarterly* 31 (Fall 1992): 85–118.
Lyons, Bonnie, and Oliver Hill. "An Interview with Bobbie Ann Mason." *Contemporary Literature* 32 (Winter 1991): 449–70.

Shomer, Enid. "An Interview with Bobbie Ann Mason." *Black Warrior Review* 12 (Spring 1986): 87–102.

Smith, Michael. "Bobbie Ann Mason, Artist and Rebel." *Kentucky Review* 8 (Autumn 1988): 56–63.

Smith Wendy. "*PW* Interviews Bobbie Ann Mason." *Publishers Weekly*, 30 August 1985, 424–25.

Wilhelm, Albert E. "An Interview with Bobbie Ann Mason." *Southern Quarterly* 26 (Winter 1988): 27–38.

Parts of Books

Barnes, Linda Adams. "The Freak Endures: The Southern Grotesque from Flannery O'Connor to Bobbie Ann Mason." In *Since Flannery O'Connor: Essays on the Contemporary Short Story*, edited by Loren Logsden and Charles W. Mayer, 133–41. Macomb: Western Illinois University Press, 1987.

Flora, Joseph M. "Bobbie Ann Mason." In *Contemporary Fiction Writers of the South*, edited by Joseph M. Flora and Robert Bain, 275–85. Westport, Conn.: Greenwood Press, 1993.

Ryan, Maureen. "Stopping Places: Bobbie Ann Mason's Short Stories." In *Women Writers of the Contemporary South*, edited by Peggy Whitman Prenshaw, 283–94. Jackson: University Press of Mississippi, 1984.

Articles

Arnold, Edwin T. "Falling Apart and Staying Together: Bobbie Ann Mason and Leon Driskell Explore the State of the Modern Family." *Appalachian Journal* 12 (Winter 1985): 135–41.

Becker, Robin. "Fear-of-Success Stories?" *Women's Review of Books* 1 (April 1984): 5–6.

Blythe, Hal, and Charlie Sweet. "The Ambiguous Grail Quest in 'Shiloh.'" *Studies in Short Fiction* 32 (Spring 1995): 223–26.

———. "Bird Imagery in Mason's 'Shiloh.'" *Notes on Contemporary Literature* 25 (November 1995): 2–3.

Brinkmeyer, Robert H. Jr. "Finding One's History: Bobbie Ann Mason and Contemporary Southern Literature." *Southern Literary Journal* 19 (Spring 1987): 22–33.

———. "Never Stop Rocking: Bobbie Ann Mason and Rock and Roll." *Mississippi Quarterly* 42 (Winter 1988–89): 5–17.

Broyard, Anatole. [a review of *Shiloh and Other Stories*]. *New York Times*, 23 November 1982, C14.

Bucher, Tina. "Changing Roles and Finding Stability: Women in Bobbie Ann Mason's *Shiloh and Other Stories*." *Border States: Journal of the Kentucky-Tennessee American Studies Association* 8 (1991): 50–55.

Conarroe, Joel. "Winning Her Father's War" [a review of *In Country*]. *New York Times Book Review*, 15 September 1985, 7.

Cooke, Steward J. "Mason's 'Shiloh.' " *Explicator* 51 (Spring 1993): 196–99.

Ditsky, John. " 'Following a Serpentine Brick Path:' The Fiction of Bobbie Ann Mason." *Hollins Critic* 33 (October 1996): 1–15.

Freeman, Judith. "Country Parables" [a review of *Love Life*]. *Los Angeles Times Book Review*, 19 March 1989, 1, 11.

Giannone, Richard. "Bobbie Ann Mason and the Recovery of Mystery." *Studies in Short Fiction* 27 (Fall 1990): 553–66.

Henning, Barbara. "Minimalism and the American Dream: 'Shiloh' by Bobbie Ann Mason and 'Preservation' by Raymond Carver." *Modern Fiction Studies* 35 (Winter 1989): 689–98.

Hill, Darlene Reimers. " 'Use to the Menfolks Would Eat First': Food and Food Rituals in the Fiction of Bobbie Ann Mason." *Southern Quarterly* 30 (Winter—Spring 1992): 81–89.

Morphew, G. O. "Downhome Feminists in *Shiloh and Other Stories*." *Southern Literary Journal* 21 (Spring 1989): 41–49.

Sheppard, R. Z. "Neighbors" [a review of *Shiloh and Other Stories*]. *Time*, 3 January 1983, 88.

Tanzman, Lea. "Mason's 'Shiloh': Another Civil War." *Notes on Contemporary Literature* 25 (September 1995): 5–6.

Thompson, Terry. "Mason's 'Shiloh.' " *Explicator* 54 (Fall 1995): 54–58.

Towers, Robert. "American Graffiti" [a review of *Shiloh and Other Stories*]. *New York Review of Books*, 16 December 1982, 38–40.

Underwood, Karen. "Mason's 'Drawing Names.' " *Explicator* 48 (Spring 1990): 231–32.

White, Leslie. "The Function of Popular Culture in Bobbie Ann Mason's *Shiloh and Other Stories* and *In Country*." *Southern Quarterly* 26 (Summer 1988): 69–79.

Wilhelm, Albert E. "Making Over or Making Off: The Problem of Identity in Bobbie Ann Mason's Short Fiction." *Southern Literary Journal* 18 (Spring 1986): 76–82.

———. "Private Rituals: Coping with Change in the Fiction of Bobbie Ann Mason." *Midwest Quarterly* 28 (Winter 1987): 271–82.

Index

26–27, 112, 137; on initiation,
29, 33–34; minimalism of, 4–6,
100, 109, 119, 137; on pastoral-
ism, 4, 47–48, 57–58; point of
view of, 28, 74, 109, 122; on popular culture, 3, 24–25, 61, 113;
on puzzles, 6, 109, 128; on quilting, 6, 97–99, 123, 128, 132; on
religion, 66, 125–26, 144–46;
Southernness of, 7–9, 47, 112,
114, 123, 137, 139; style of,
120–21, 131; on television, 29,
67–68, 71, 94–95, 113, 121;
word play of, 128–29; writing
process of, 11, 48, 87, 109, 111,
118, 125, 131

WORKS: NONFICTION BOOKS
Girl Sleuth, The, 6
Nabokov's Garden: A Guide to Ada, 59,
122

WORKS: NONFICTION ESSAYS
"Creating Meaning out of the
Chaos," 87, 109
"Way We Lived, The," 7–8

WORKS: NOVELS
Feather Crowns, 75, 133
In Country, 7, 60, 73, 83, 86, 111,
114, 117, 120, 152, 154, 159–61
Spence + Lila, 18, 27, 37, 41, 56, 72,
110, 111, 113, 122

WORKS: SHORT STORIES
"Big Bertha Stories," 60, 81, 83–86
"Blue Country," 41
"Bumblebees," 51, 54–58, 101,
125
"Climber, The," 3, 155
"Coyotes," 60, 70, 79–83, 91
"Detroit Skyline, 1949," 10, 28–33,
34, 35, 38, 120, 124
"Drawing Names," 4, 14, 25–28, 72
"Hunktown," 48, 49, 51–54, 57
"Love Life," 3, 60, 94–99, 122, 127
"Lying Doggo," 3, 41–43, 70, 80
"Marita," 73–76, 122

"Memphis," 17–21, 28, 37, 46, 113,
127
"Midnight Magic," 10–13, 14, 42,
60, 80, 100, 101, 125
"Nancy Culpepper," 38–41, 70, 80,
99, 156
"New-Wave Format, A," 61, 90–94,
95, 156–58
"Ocean, The," 10, 35–38, 60, 120
"Offerings," 48–51, 57
"Old Things," 15, 27, 60, 69–73
"Piano Fingers," 86–90
"Residents and Transients," 43–46,
57, 71, 87, 96, 154, 156
"Retreat, The," 66, 140, 143–46
"Rookers, The," 60, 65–69, 72, 100,
155
"Running Around," 10
"Secret of the Pyramids, The,"
21–25, 28, 32
"Shiloh," 14, 15, 35, 60, 61–65, 66,
72, 88, 100, 109, 123, 126, 131,
140–43, 148
"Sorghum," 13–17, 18, 20, 25, 28,
47, 72, 100
"State Champions," 33–35, 116
"Still Life with Watermelon," 48, 60,
76–79
"Third Monday," 138–39, 140,
146–50
"Wish," 127

WORKS: SHORT STORY COLLECTIONS
Love Life, 109, 111, 120, 122, 124,
125
Shiloh and Other Stories, 8, 41, 71,
109, 111, 120, 124, 139, 150,
154–58, 162

Mason, LaNelle, 110
Mason, Samuel, 7
Melville, Herman, 131; *Moby Dick,*
131
"Memphis," 17–21, 28, 37, 46, 113,
127
"Midnight Magic," 10–13, 14, 42,
60, 80, 100, 101, 125
Mississippi Review, 4

The Author

Albert Wilhelm received a Ph.D. in English from the University of North Carolina at Chapel Hill and taught at Morehouse College and Duke University before becoming a professor of English at Tennessee Technological University. He has served as a Fulbright lecturer on American literature at Marie Curie University in Lublin, Poland, and at Seoul National University in Korea. He has published scholarly articles on Bobbie Ann Mason and on several other American writers including Thomas Wolfe, Robert Penn Warren, John Updike, and Joseph Heller.

The Editors

Gary Scharnhorst is professor of English at the University of New Mexico, coeditor of *American Literary Realism,* and editor in alternating years of *American Literary Scholarship: An Annual.* He is the author or editor of books about Horatio Alger Jr., Charlotte Perkins Gilman, Bret Harte, Nathaniel Hawthorne, Henry David Thoreau, and Mark Twain, and he has taught in Germany on Fulbright fellowships three times (1978–1979, 1985–1986, 1993). He is also the current president of the Western Literature Association and the Pacific Northwest American Studies Association.

Eric Haralson is assistant professor of English at the State University of New York at Stony Brook. He has published articles on American and English literature—in *American Literature, Nineteenth-Century Literature,* the *Arizona Quarterly, American Literary Realism,* and the *Henry James Review,* as well as in several essay collections. He is also the editor of *The Garland Encyclopedia of American Nineteenth-Century Poetry.*